# AC ELECTRIC LOCOMOTIVES

## in Colour

## Gavin Morrison

Ian Allan

PUBLISHING

First published 2013

ISBN 978 0 7110 3505 8

Published by Ian Allan Publishing
an imprint of Ian Allan Publishing Ltd, Hersham, Surrey, KT12 4RG

Printed in Malta

Distributed in the United States of America and Canada by BookMasters Distribution Services

Visit the Ian Allan Publishing website at
**www.ianallanpublishing.com**

*Front cover, top:* No 86218 *Planet* on a down express just south of Tring station, 19 April 1982. *Gavin Morrison*

*Front cover, bottom:* No 90040 *The Railway Mission*, in EWS livery, heads the 15.40 Warrington–Willesden vans approaching Linslade tunnel. *Gavin Morrison*

*Back cover:* No 87013 *John O'Gaunt* waits to leave London Euston on a down express on 21 February 2001. *Gavin Morrison*

*Previous page:* Brand new Class 90 No 90049, almost complete and painted in Railfreight Distribution livery, is seen inside Crewe Works on 13 August 1990 before entering service. It worked its first train on 20 October 1990. It was renumbered 90149 on 16 July 1991, but was altered back to 90049 on 4 September 2002. It is currently working in the Freightliner fleet. *Gavin Morrison*

# CONTENTS

# INTRODUCTION

I am delighted to have been given the opportunity to compile this colour album of the AC electric locomotives, which I have always felt received far less coverage in the railway press, than the diesel classes. I am not sure why this is the case, but it may be that photographers prefer to take pictures on lines without the electrification masts and wires, or that the number of routes where there is AC locomotive haulage are few.

Apart from the Southern third-rail routes, electrification of our railways has been very slow, compared to Europe and some other countries. The DC 'locomotive' era has long since passed into history, except for the few Class 73s still in service.

It was back in 1956 when the government turned its thoughts to electrification, but there was no experience in this county of building AC traction and many people in power were very nervous of investing so much of the taxpayers' money in relatively unknown technology. The apparent benefits obtained on the SNCF specifications convinced the government to go ahead with a pilot scheme, which was the 42 miles from Manchester to Crewe. Five different manufacturers were given orders to provide locomotives to their design, but incorporating a standard cab layout. One hundred locomotives were ordered, Classes AL1 to AL5 (later Classes 81 to 85); the same policy had been done with diesel classes, resulting in some good and some troublesome results. More details are given in the introduction to the classes.

As explained later in the book, testing and crew training was carried out on the nine miles between Wilmslow and Slade Green Junction via Style, with the former gas turbine No 18100 converted to AC electric.

The eventual outcome of the prototypes AL1 to AL5, was the AL6 (Class 86) which became the reliable backbone of West Coast traction for many decades, even after the introduction of the Class 87 and 90s. Forty-eight years after the Class 86s entered service they can still be seen on the West Coast main line and in Anglia working freightliners, while others, as well as the Class 87s, have been sold abroad for further use.

It took another 15 years after the opening of the Manchester–Crewe section before electrification was completed right through between Euston and Glasgow and the full benefits could be gained and most of the locomotive

*Below:* On the crisp afternoon of 26 November 1996, the cooling towers of Drax power station make an impressive backdrop to this picture of InterCity-liveried Class 91 No 91011 heading north at Burn when it was named *Terence Cuneo*. The plates were removed in May 1997, but the name was re-applied in sticker form in June 2000. It was delivered new to Bounds Green depot on 2 March 1990, and re-entered service after major refurbishment on 12 December 2002 renumbered 91111. It was the only member of the class to receive National Express livery. *Gavin Morrison*

classes gave excellent and reliable service over the years until the arrival of the Pendolinos, which finally ousted the locomotives in June 2005. Most of the prototypes managed to continue in service until the late 1980s and early 1990s.

It was around another 15 years before the Class 91s appeared for the East Coast electrification and they have now put in around 25 years' service. In 1993 to 1996 the very powerful and complex Class 92s appeared, which have been badly underutilised ever since their introduction. Even today there is usually only about half of the class active at any one time.

I have tried, in this album, to show all the classes working on different services on which AC locomotives have been used over the years, and to give basic technical details on each class.

Since sectorisation there has been an explosion of different liveries much to the delight of enthusiast photographers.,

My thanks must go to the photographers who have helped me out with gaps in my collection, but particularly Mike Mensing, who had the foresight to photograph the AL1 to AL6s in the early days. Without his help it would have been very difficult to give a balanced picture.

*Above:* Class 85 No 85037 heading an up Larbert–Oakleigh calcium carbonate train as it passes the well-known photographic location of Beckfoot in the Cumberland fells near Low Gill on 26 May 1990. When it entered BR stock on 5 February 1964 it was numbered E3092. It continued in service until withdrawn on 3 September 1990, and was broken up at MC Metal processing Springburn Works on 11 October 1992. *Gavin Morrison*

Due to various reasons the book publication date was rescheduled, and I felt it necessary to add an additional eight pages, which show the liveries that have appeared on the various classes since the book was originally presented. I am grateful to Ian Allan for agreeing to these extra pages, which will make the book up-to-date, I hope, when published, although this cannot be guaranteed.

I hope the album brings back happy memories, of an era which seems to be currently fading, but who knows, may reappear in the future.

Gavin Morrison
*December 2012*

## Bibliography

*'Sparks', A Celebration of British AC Electric Locomotives,* Charles Buchan, Triangle Publishing 2006, ISBN 0-9550030-1-6
*Allocation History of BR Diesel and Electrics, 3rd and final edition,* Roger Harris, March 2004
*Power of the AC Electrics,* Brian Morrison, Oxford Publishing Co, 1988, ISBN 0-86096-246-X

*Right:* A Wembley–Mossend car-carrying train passes Carpenders Park at 17.47 on 8 June 2005, hauled by Class 92 No 92025 *Oscar Wilde*. Its construction was completed in January 1995, but it didn't enter service until the following September. Originally it was a Railfreight Distribution locomotive, but passed to EWS ownership at privatisation. It is now part of the DB Schenker fleet, still carrying its original grey livery. *Gavin Morrison*

# THE FIRST AC LOCOMOTIVE ON BRITISH RAILWAYS

**Built:** 1951

**Built by:** Metropolitan-Vickers as a gas turbine locomotive

**Withdrawn:** 1958

**Conversion:** To AC electric between January and October 1958

**Converted by:** Metropolitan-Vickers / Beyer Peacock, Stockton-on-Tees

**Number built:** 1

**Weight:** 109 tons

**Designed max hp:** 2,500

**Max speed:** 90mph

**Withdrawn:** 1968

It is often thought that the first BR AC electric locomotive was Class AL1 (later Class 81) No E3001, which was introduced in November 1959, but in fact it was Metropolitan-Vickers-built gas turbine locomotive No 18100, built for the Western Region which had become surplus to requirements and was withdrawn in January 1958, and then converted into an AC locomotive. It emerged fitted with vacuum brakes, pneumatic sanding gear and electric train heating (ETH) with a wheel arrangement of A1A-A1A, with much of the original equipment being reused. Its maximum speed was 90mph.

The cab layout was totally redesigned to make it similar to the design chosen for the Class AL1 to AL5 prototype electrics. A novel feature was the creation of a small room at the No 1 end, which was used as an on-board classroom.

When it entered service in October 1958, it was rated at 2,500hp, weighing 109 tons, with a tractive effort of 40,000lb.

One of the prime reasons for its conversion was to get drivers trained before the Class AL1 to AL5s arrived, which were still 15-18 months hence, and this it did very successfully using the Style line, which was little used at the time.

Its original number of 18100 was altered to E1000, this being changed again to E2000 in October 1959.

It is claimed that by 1960 it had trained 1,300 drivers, so that when the Manchester–Crewe section was opened in September 1960 electric services were able to start, followed by the Crewe–Liverpool section in January 1962. No E2000 spent some time in the Liverpool area.

As the new electric locomotives were placed into service, No E2000 found itself with little work, but was sent to Scotland for a very short period as a test vehicle for the newly electrified Glasgow suburban lines before services started. Eventually it was sent to the Rugby test plant for long-term storage.

It was used again in 1964 around Rugby for driver training but soon returned to storage.

The end came in April 1968, and it was taken to Market Harborough where it languished until 1972, being sold for scrap that November to J. Cashmore Ltd who broke it up in 1973.

Under TOPS it was classified as a Class 80, although TOPS only became operational in 1974. It certainly deserved to be preserved, but unfortunately that didn't happen.

*Below:* The Metropolitan Vickers gas turbine is shown after conversion to AC electric locomotive E1000. *Colin Marsden*

# CLASS AL1 / 81

| | |
|---|---|
| **Original Numbers:** E3001-23, E3301-2 | |
| **Built:** 1959-64 | |
| **Number built:** 25 | |
| **Contracted to:** Associated Electrical Industries (AEI) Ltd | |
| Mechanically constructed by: Birmingham Railway Carriage & Wagon (BRCW) | |
| **Weight:** 79 tons | |
| **Designed max hp:** 4,800 | |
| **Max speed:** 100mph | |
| **Withdrawn:** | |

No E3001 (later No 81001) was the first of the five AC electric locomotive prototypes to enter service in November 1959.

Rectifiers were fitted to the class, although there was no previous experience of fitting them to locomotives in the UK, other than the experience gained from No E2000. Mercury-arc-type rectifiers were used to convert the AC power supply into DC current to feed to the traction motors. A 'tap' control allowed the driver to increase or decrease power by 'notching up' or 'notching down'. Two Stone-Faiveley single-arm pantographs were used to collect current from the overhead wires, both being able to accept 6.25Kv as well as 25kV; this was due to perceived safety issues on limited clearances with 25kV.

The body design had nine ventilation grilles on the side plus four non-opening windows, and was painted in Electric Blue livery. With a raked-back nose end, it offered a very modern appearance for 1959.

Eight of the class had been completed by the time the Manchester–Crewe line went live, others following together with the AL2, AL3 and AL4s. Two of the class had a type B specification, limiting them for freight-only use. The first numbered E3301 entered traffic with the type B specification but was soon altered to type A, whilst the other, No E3302, was altered during construction. They were both renumbered to E3096 and E3097, eventually becoming Nos 81021 and 81022.

The locomotives were used on all types of traffic on the first electrified sections, but once electrification reached Euston in 1966 they were able to show their true capabilities between Manchester, Liverpool and the capital.

They were not without faults; one that became apparent was the rough riding, which was never really cured, but improved by extra maintenance. The mercury-arc rectifiers gave trouble, but not as badly as the other prototypes; this of course added to maintenance costs, eventually resulting in the decision to replace them with silver diode-type in the late 1970s. As these modifications were done in the works, the locomotives emerged numbered as Class 81s. Dual-braking was also fitted during this period.

By the end of the 1970s the class was mainly confined to freight workings north of Crewe, as the Class 87s, along with the 100 Class 86s, were now fully operational. The class was allocated to Shields Road depot in Glasgow and they had their maximum speed reduced to 80mph.

The end came for the class when the Class 90s were built but by then they had put in 30 years of service; a good performance for a prototype design. Fortunately No 81002 (E3003) survived into preservation.

*Left:* No 81011 (E3011) along with other locomotives is seen inside the purpose-built depot at Willesden on 31 July 1977. *Gavin Morrison*

*Left:* A fine picture of Class AL1 No E3021 (later No 81018) climbing away from Runcorn on 20 July 1963 with the 4.20pm service from Liverpool Lime Street–Euston, which also conveyed the 2.50pm portion from Southport. After catching fire in September 1985 it was stored and withdrawn in January 1986, although it wasn't until July 1992 that it was cut up at MC Metal Processing at Glasgow. *Mike Mensing*

*Right:* The first of the AL1s, No E3001 (later No 81001) heads the up 9.55am Holyhead–Euston past Easenhall to the north of Rugby on the Trent Valley line on 24 August 1968. It caught fire whilst working the 11.15am Euston–Stirling Motorail train near Carstairs on 26 August 1983, but it was not withdrawn until 29 July 1974 and was not cut up until September 1986 at Crewe Works. *Mike Mensing*

*Left:* Class 81 No 81011 is hauling an up freight of flat wagons past Portobello junction east of Wolverhampton on the Grand Junction main line on 21 November 1975. The junction can be seen in the distance, the left going to Wolverhampton and the right to Bushbury. No 81011 (ex E3013) was withdrawn on 5 April 1989 and cut up at Coopers Metals in Sheffield in December 1991. *Mike Mensing*

*Above:* On 22 October 1983 No 81017 (E3020) is just south of Crewe station heading an up freightliner. It is about to pass the carriage sheds on the right, which are just out of the picture. The locomotive was one of the last two of the class to be withdrawn in June 1991. *Gavin Morrison*

*Below:* Just south of Basford Hall yards at Crewe, No 81019 (E3022) is seen on the down slow line heading a freight that is just about to enter the yards. Seen on 31 May 1983, this locomotive lasted in service until January 1989. *Gavin Morrison*

*Left:* On a summer Saturday, 1 June 1985, No 81018 (E3021) has been pressed into service on a passenger working. It has been stopped at the signal to the south end of Crewe alongside the carriage sheds. It was withdrawn in January 1986. *Gavin Morrison*

*Right:* The West Coast main line north of Wigan used to be four-track, but had been reduced to two by the time this photograph was taken on 10 May 1982. No 81020 (E3023) is heading north past Charnock Richard with a freightliner for Mossend. No 81020 was withdrawn in July 1987. *Gavin Morrison*

*Left:* Class 81 No 81007 heads north on the slow line between Warrington and Winwick Junction on 3 July 1982. It was No E3007 when new in July 1960 but went into store for two months before entering service. It suffered fire damage at Carstairs on 6 December 1985 but was repaired and continued in service until 3 October 1988. It was eventually scrapped in January 1992 at Coopers Metals, Attercliffe. *Gavin Morrison*

*Left:* The north end of Nuneaton station on 3 April 1986 sees No 81011 (E3013) on an up express for Euston. In the background the avoiding line can just be seen on the top of the embankment. Nuneaton has now been remodelled and new platforms built to the right of the picture, so Leicester–Birmingham services don't have to cross the main lines. *Gavin Morrison*

*Right:* The fells above Tebay in the background are nearly lost in the haze on 17 October 1986. No 81003 (E3004) is passing Greenholme with a down express heading for Shap summit, which is another 2½ miles to the north at 916ft. No 81003 remained in service until March 1988. *Gavin Morrison*

*Left:* No E3003 (81002) was the member of the AL1/Class 81 which was selected for preservation, having been withdrawn in October 1990. It is seen here on 28 August 1995 attending an open day in Basford Hall yards and is painted in BR Electric Blue livery. *Gavin Morrison*

AC ELECTRIC LOCOMOTIVES in colour

# CLASS AL2 / 82

| | |
|---|---|
| **Original Numbers:** E3046-55 | |
| **Built:** May 1960 to April 1962 | |
| **Number built:** 10 | |
| **Contracted to:** Metropolitan-Vickers (Metro-Vick) (part of AEI) | |
| Sub-contracted to: Beyer Peacock, Gorton, Manchester | |
| **Weight:** 80 tons | |
| **Designed max hp:** 5,500 (continuous 3,300hp) | |
| **Max tractive effort:** 50,000lb | |
| **Max speed:** 100mph | |
| **Withdrawn:** September 1969 to December 1987 | |

Beyer Peacock had a reputation for producing well-built steam and diesel locomotives, but had little experience with electrics. Being part of the AEI group, it was no surprise that Metro-Vick decided to use as many parts as it could that were being used in the Class AL1 (81). The sturdier construction than the 'AL1s' put them at the weight limit for BR specifications, this after a lightweight alloy and fibreglass had been used in the construction. Whilst similar in design to the 'AL1s', the 'AL2s' differed in that the body side had six louvre openings on one side only and two on the other side plus two non-opening windows. Two Stone-Faiveley single-arm pantographs were fitted and, like the 'AL1s', could collect 6.25Kv or 25kV, although the last of the class had a cross-arm design to test which type was better at collecting current. Although successful, the locomotive was refitted with the original style pantographs.

Electric train heating (ETH) was fitted, along with APC (automatic power control). No E3046 left the works

at Gorton in May 1960 and was tested on the Style line, and by April 1962 all ten locomotives had been delivered.

The 'AL2s' became more popular with the crews than the 'AL1s', mainly because they had a smoother ride and more power. Again the mercury-arc rectifiers gave trouble with flashovers, but were much better than what was experienced with the 'AL3' and 'AL4s'. Because they had fewer ventilation louvres on the bodyside, they were prone to overheat when the electrical equipment was running when stationary. It was as early as 1966 when No E3055 caught fire and was considered beyond economical repair.

Like other classes they were fitted with dual braking apparatus, room for the required reservoir being provided by the space vacated by the second pantograph. Eventually the mercury-arc rectifiers were exchanged for the more reliable silicon-diode type, when an additional grille was added to the body side.

With the completion of the electrification to Glasgow in May 1974, the class put in some useful work on the main expresses prior to the delivery of the Class 87s.

In the 1990s they found themselves more involved with freight and parcels workings, having been pushed out by the Class 86 and 87s. No 82002 was stored in October 1981, and the last two, Nos 82005 and 82008 by November 1982. Nos 82005 and 82008 were reprieved for use working the empty stock movements in and out of Euston. By the end of 1987 they were withdrawn, the ECS duties being taken over by surplus Class 81s. Thus ended 27 years of good service, compared to some of the other prototypes.

*Left:* Looking immaculate after repainting into BR blue livery, No 82008 is at the Basford Hall yard open day on 21 August 1994. Originally No E3054 when built in November 1961, it was loaned to the Rugby electric depot in August 1963 where it was used for driver training. It was stored in August 1982 at Longsight depot but reinstated in May 1983 for use on empty stock movements between Euston and Stonebridge Park carriage sidings, becoming the only member of the class to be painted into InterCity livery. It was withdrawn on 18 December 1987 and was eventually bought by Pete Waterman, who then sold it to the AC Traction Group. *Gavin Morrison*

*Above:* No 82002 (E3048) is on a down main line passenger duty approaching Stowe Hill tunnel (491yd) between Roade and Rugby on 9 September 1978. Introduced in August 1960, it lasted until August 1983. It had been out of service since 19 June 1980 when it received serious fire damage. It was moved to Crewe Works and repairs started, and it was said the repair costs had exceeded £100,000, but by then BR decided that damaged prototype locomotives should be withdrawn. It was eventually broken up at the Berry's yard towards the end on 1984. *Gavin Morrison*

*Below:* In the summer of 1981 there was a fairly regular Class 82 working on a semi-fast train from Crewe to Preston, returning at around 17.00. On 24 August 1981 No 82008 is shown heading north at Charnock Richard, a few miles north of Wigan, where there used to be four tracks. The locomotive is running with the indicator panel plated over. *Gavin Morrison*

# CLASS AL3 / 83

| | |
|---|---|
| **Original Numbers:** | E3024-35, E3098-E3100, E3303-4 |
| **Built:** | May 1960 to June 1962 |
| **Number built:** | 15 |
| **Contracted to:** | English Electric |
| **Built at:** | Vulcan Foundry, Newton-le-Willows |
| **Weight:** | 77 tons |
| **Designed max hp:** | continuous 2,950 |
| **Max tractive effort:** | 38,000lb |
| **Max speed:** | 100mph |
| **Withdrawn:** | May 1975 to March 1989 |

English Electric had a reputation for building fine diesel locomotives, e.g. Classes 08, 37 and 40, so it was fair to assume that the same would apply to an electric product. Time was to prove that this was to be far from the case.

The AL3s were lighter than the other prototypes and less powerful. The first example, No E3024, appeared in July 1960.

Weight reduction was one of the company's prime objectives, and to this end used special 'Cortes' steel for the bodywork and many other features, which it was argued made them cheaper to build. It was claimed that an 'AL3' cost £50,000 compared to a 'Deltic' at £200,000. This obviously appealed to the BR management. Two of the class were to be of a freight specification (type B previously mentioned) and were duly delivered for 80mph operation and numbered E3303 and E3304. The last of the class No E3100 was to be a test-bed locomotive, delivered with silicon-arc rectifiers, and valuable information was gained with wheel-slip protection, control of tractive effort and rheostatic braking. The locomotive was eventually stored after the testing in April 1969. The other two type B locomotives

were converted to 100mph capability.

Again the mercury-arc rectifiers gave trouble, but more so with the 'AL3s' than the other classes, to such an extent that the whole class was stored in the winter of 1968/69, together with the troublesome 'AL4s'. Fortunately the Class AL6s were now around, so services could be run without them.

As already mentioned, the electrification extension to Glasgow, announced in 1970, created a potential shortage of power, so a decision was taken to install silicon-diode rectifiers to every member of the class, which was carried out at Doncaster Works. Class AL4 (84) No E3046 had been extensively tested before the decision was taken.

In the mid-1980s new locomotives became available; the lack of power in the Class AL3s (83) was considered a drawback, especially as trains were becoming heavier, so apart from accident early withdrawals, the others started to be taken out of service in March 1981.

Like the two Class 82s, Nos 83012 and 83015 joined the '82s' on empty stock duties at Euston and were later joined by No 83009. No 83012 received InterCity livery and was eventually preserved by Pete Waterman; like the Class 82 it ended up with the AC Locomotive Group.

Looking back on the class history and performance, I am sure English Electric wished they had never been associated with the 'AL3s'.

*Below:* No 83010 (originally E3033) is seen out of use and stored at Longsight shed on 30 September 1982. Alongside others of the class, it was moved to Stockport carriage sidings in October 1983 and then to Cockshute Yard at Stoke-on-Trent for continued storage. Its end came at the Berry's yard at Leicester in December 1984. *Gavin Morrison*

*Above:* No E3035 is at Easenhall between Rugby and Nuneaton at the head of the 14.05 Euston–Glasgow Central on 24 August 1968. It became No 83012, and was stored at Bury in April 1969. Three years later it was sent to Doncaster Works for modification. It was stored again at Allerton in February 1982, then at Longsight. Surprisingly it was reinstated in 1993 for empty stock duties in and out of Euston until it passed into preservation in December 1992, having been withdrawn in March 1989. *Mike Mensing*

*Above:* The first of Class 83 (AL3), No 83001 (originally E3024) heads an up freight past Atherstone station on the Trent Valley line on 23 July 1975. *Mike Mensing*

*Above:* No 83002 (originally E3025) arriving at Nuneaton station with the 10.52 Blackpool North–Euston on 21 August 1976. Like other classmates it was stored at Bury shed in 1969 until refurbished in 1972. After collision damage in 1981 it was stored after repairs were discovered to be too expensive and withdrawn in July 1983. It went to Vic Berry's and was cut up by December 1984. *Mike Mensing*

*Left:* Details of No 83010 seen here have been given on page 13. It is shown arriving at Lichfield station on 21 August 1976 with an up InterCity express and passing the signalbox situated between the up and down lines. *Mike Mensing*

*Right:* A night shot in Basford Hall yard, taken on 20 August 1994, prior to an open day sees No 83012 (E3035) painted into the InterCity livery, which it received when employed on empty stock duties out of Euston. It was given this repaint in 1986 and was the only member of the class to receive this livery, It was withdrawn in March 1989 and saved for preservation by Pete Waterman. *Gavin Morrison*

*Left:* By the time of the Old Oak Common open day on 6 August 2000, No 83012 had been repainted into its original Electric Blue livery and renumbered E3035. The immaculate locomotive is shown at this event. *Gavin Morrison*

# CLASS AL4 / 84

| | |
|---|---|
| **Original Numbers:** E3036-45 | |
| **Built:** March 1960 to March 1961 | |
| **Number built:** 10 | |
| **Contracted to:** North British Locomotive Co / General Electric Co | |
| **Built at:** Hyde Park Works, Glasgow | |
| **Weight:** 77 tons | |
| **Designed max hp:** continuous 3,300 | |
| **Max tractive effort:** 50,000lb | |
| **Max speed:** 100mph | |
| **Withdrawn:** April 1977 to November 1980 | |

The North British Locomotive Co (NBL) constructed the class at its Hyde Park Works in Glasgow and General Electric Co Ltd provided the electrical components.

No E3036 left the works in March 1960, looking similar to the other prototypes but with oval buffers and recessed route indicator panels.

Once in traffic many faults emerged, which included flashovers in the transformer windings, short lifespan for the motor spring drives, major problems with the rectifiers and rough riding. As early as April 1963 the class was taken out of traffic and after attempts to solve the problems others appeared when they returned to traffic. By October/November 1967 the whole class was back in store at Bury. Had it not been for the announcement of the extension of the electrification to Glasgow, they would probably have been withdrawn. It was apparent that they would be needed for the extra services so a decision was taken in May 1968 to reinstate No E3043 (84008). It was sent to the Rugby Testing Station and eventually it was decided to replace the unreliable 'Com-Pak' rectifiers with silicon-diode ones, the rest of the class being altered by May 1972. Even after all this money had been spent on the class they still gave trouble in service, mainly with the traction motors.

As the Class 87s entered service, the opportunity to sideline the Class 84s was soon taken, with Nos 84005 and 84007 going in April 1977.

No 84001 entered preservation at the National Railway Museum, whilst No 84009 was modified and became departmental No ADB968021; it lasted as a testing vehicle until 1992 and was then scrapped, although one cab was preserved. So ended the career of probably the least successful of the prototype locomotives.

*Below:* One month before its withdrawal No 84003 (E3038) is at the east end of Birmingham New Street station awaiting its next duty on 25 August 1980. *Gavin Morrison*

*Left:* Class AL4, No E3045 (84010), was only three months old when this picture was taken on 24 June 1961, but already appears to be out of use and dumped at the back of Longsight depot. It is in the original blue livery and became the last of the class. *Gavin Morrison*

*Right:* Class AL4 No E3042 (84007) is heading the 11.10am Manchester–Cardiff/ Paignton on the approach to Crewe on 5 March 1961. A generator coach is seen behind the locomotive, which is only five months old. *Mike Mensing*

*Left:* At the head of a down freight carrying cars, No 84004 (originally E3039) heads north at Polesworth on the Trent Valley line on 12 September 1977. It was stored at Bury in October 1967 and headed to Doncaster Works for modifications in September 1971. It was eventually withdrawn in November 1977, but was not actually cut up until April 1985 by Birds Commercial Motors at Long Marston. *Mike Mensing*

*Left:* A lightweight parcels working for No 84008 (originally E3043) as it heads south near Mancetter on the Trent Valley line south of Atherstone on 16 September 1978. Like other members of the class it was stored at Bury shed in November 1967. It was taken to Rugby Testing Station in May 1968, but no testing seems to have taken place. Moved to Doncaster Works in January 1971 and refurbished, it was back in store between January 1974 and July 1976 and was withdrawn in October 1979. It was put into departmental stock but not used, and was eventually broken up at Newcastle-under-Lyme in November 1988 after a very unsuccessful career. *Mike Mensing*

*Right:* Preserved No 84001 (E3036) is shown attending Crewe Electric Depot open day along with many other electric locomotives on 15 October 1994. *Gavin Morrison*

*Left:* Ex-No 84009 (E3044) but now part of the Railway Technical centre at Derby as a mobile load bank. Numbered ADB968021, it entered service as an unpowered machine in October 1979, and outlived its other classmates by a considerable margin, not being officially withdrawn until December 1992. One of its cabs has been preserved by the AC Locomotive Group. It was being exhibited at Crewe Electric Depot's open day. *Gavin Morrison*

# CLASS AL5 / 85

| | |
|---|---|
| **Original Numbers:** E3056-95 | |
| **Built:** August 1961 to December 1964 | |
| **Number built:** 40 | |
| **Contracted to:** BR Doncaster Works / AEI | |
| **Weight:** 83 tons | |
| **Continuous rating:** 3,200hp (max 5,100hp) | |
| **Max tractive effort:** 50,000lb | |
| **Max speed:** 100mph | |
| **Withdrawn:** July 1983 to November 1992 | |

The Class AL5s (85) were the only class of the prototypes to be built in BR workshops, and Doncaster was the location selected. Again AEI supplied the electrical equipment.

Much experience had been gained from the 'AL1' and 'AL2' classes, which was used in the 'AL5s'; one feature that differed from the other classes was the lightweight upper body section, which was able to be removed to give better access for maintenance. Another difference was the fitting of rheostatic electric braking equipment.

The first of the class, No E3057, entered service in June 1961 along with No E3058. The class settled down well after a few teething problems had been sorted out.

They were employed on top link work, where once again poor riding qualities showed. Another problem area was the germanium rectifiers on the earlier members of the class, but these were replaced. Air brakes were eventually fitted, and like the other classes the air reservoirs took the place of the redundant second pantograph.

Until the arrival of the Class 87s in 1973-4 the class was to be seen working the top Anglo-Scottish expresses, but gradually they were utilised more on Speedlink duties, mainly on the northern section of the West Coast main line. No 85027 (E3082) was withdrawn after an accident in May 1983, but it wasn't until 1989 that BR decided to stop repairs on the class.

A change of policy in 1989 resulted in the best eleven members of the class being given overhauls and modified for freight duties. These were done between June 1989 and October 1990, and they were reclassified Class 85/1, and limited to 75mph. When the Class 90s arrived in 1988, plus the modified Class 86s for freight duties, the Class 85s did not last long on the main line, No 85111 being withdrawn in March 1990. As with other prototype classes, four finished up on ECS duties, Nos 85018 and 85040 plus Nos 85101 and 85110. No 85101 was the final one to be withdrawn in November 1991 when it passed into preservation.

*Below:* No 85024 (E3079) is shown inside Crewe ETD on 27 February 1988. The following year it was modified to No 85107 and continued in service until May 1990. *Gavin Morrison*

*Left:* The 9.40am Perth–Euston is one mile south of Polesworth on the Trent Valley line, headed by No E3071 (later No 85016, and then 85105) on 24 August 1968. It was withdrawn on 8 July 1991 and moved to Metal Processing, Glasgow, for cutting-up in September 1992. *Mike Mensing*

*Right:* No 85032 (originally E3087) is stabled at the south end of Springs Branch depot awaiting its next duty on 14 June 1982. This locomotive, like many others, suffered fire damage, sustained at Beattock summit on 9 December 1988, which proved too expensive to repair and it was withdrawn on 19 February 1989. After storage it was eventually cut up at MC Metals, Glasgow. *Gavin Morrison*

*Left:* No 85002 (originally E3057) has just passed Lichfield Trent Valley station with a down car train on 14 May 1979. It survived until 17 May 1989, but over three years passed before it was broken up by MC Metal Processing, Glasgow, in October 1992. *Mike Mensing*

*Above:* In superb evening lighting No E3056 (later No 85001), the first of Class AL5, heads north on the 'Emerald Isle Express', the 5.40pm Euston–Holyhead just south of Polesworth on 18 August 1968. It was another Class 85 which caught fire, this time on 13 October 1985 near South Kenton whilst working the 16.15 Euston–Manchester. It was too expensive to repair and so was eventually cut up by MC Metal Processing in April 1989. *Mike Mensing*

*Below:* A powerful picture of No E3083 (later No 85028) heading the down evening 'Executive', 1G70, the 5.50pm Euston–Wolverhampton High Level near Hampton in Arden on 22 August 1968. Details of the locomotive are given on page 24. *Mike Mensing*

*Right:* No 85027 (E3082) is at the head of a northbound freightliner approaching Springs Branch, Wigan, on 14 June 1982. Ten months after this picture was taken the locomotive suffered severe fire damage near Kings Langley, while working an up Ford container train. The cost of repairs was considered too high, so it became the first of the class to be withdrawn on 17 July 1983. It was scrapped at Crewe Works. *Gavin Morrison*

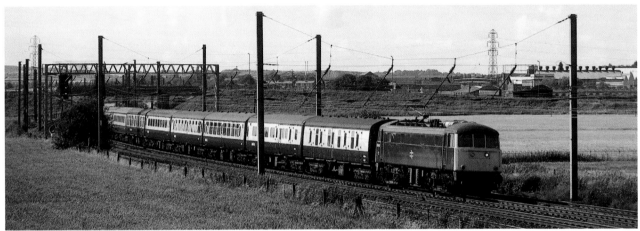

*Above:* A fantastic location for enthusiasts to watch the activity on the West Coast main line is Winwick junction, just north of Warrington, where No 85019 (originally E3074) is powering an up express on 3 July 1982. Its career ended on 1 December 1989, and it was scrapped by Vic Berry at Leicester in November 1990. *Gavin Morrison*

*Below:* No 85020 (E3075) is approaching Manchester Piccadilly with a down express on 8 June 1984. The locomotive had a premature end when hauling 6S73, the 10.26 Dover-Mossend speedlink service on 27 February 1989, when it ran into the rear of the 6E26 Warrington–Doncaster speedlink at Walton Old Junction yard, Warrington. It suffered severe cab damage and after 18 months the decision was taken to withdraw it on 17 October 1990. It was also cut up at MC Metals, Glasgow. *Gavin Morrison*

*Left:* Top link work for No 85005 (E3060), shown leaving Crewe on the down 'Manchester Pullman' on 1 June 1985. The photograph was taken one day before Crewe closed down for major reorganisation. The locomotive was stored on 18 September 1989 and withdrawn on 25 May 1990. It was scrapped on 28 January 1993 at MC Metals, Glasgow. *Gavin Morrison*

*Right:* This picture was taken from the A74 road just south of Crawford and shows the Hardendale–Ravenscraig heading north hauled by No 85022 (E3081) on 7 June 1988. *Gavin Morrison*

*Left:* The 1S64 8.33am Paignton–Glasgow Central headed by No 85005 (E3090) passes rapidly by Beattock at the start of the 10-mile climb to the summit of 1,015ft on 22 September 1988. The old steam shed for the banking engines was just to the right of the picture, at the end of the train. It closed in 1967. *Gavin Morrison*

*Left:* No 85028 (E3083) is at Euston station on ECS duties on 8 April 1989. Also in the picture is Class 90 No 90005 and Class 86/4 No 86431. No 85028 was withdrawn on 10 January 1990, eight months after this picture was taken. After 3½ years it arrived at MC Metals, Glasgow, and was cut-up on 25 May 1994, and became the last of the class to survive by six months. *Gavin Morrison*

*Right:* No 85106 (originally E3076, then No 85021) passes Ripple Lane yard with one Ford wagon on 29 March 1990. This was another Class 85 (AL5) to end its career due to fire damage, whilst working 4M58 Southampton–Trafford Park freightliner near Soho, Birmingham, on 15 October 1990, It only ran as No 85106 from July 1989. Its end came at MC Metals, Glasgow, on 29 September 1992. *Gavin Morrison*

*Left:* No 85103 (originally E3065, then No 85010) is heading north on a down freight just south of Basford Hall yard at Crewe on 20 July 1990. As already explained in other captions many Class 85s were withdrawn due to fire or accident damage, and No 85103 was no exception. It suffered underframe damage due to a collision in Bescot yard on 13 May 1991, after becoming No 85103 in July 1989. Like many others in the class it was broken up at MC Metals, Glasgow, on 11 September 1992. *Gavin Morrison*

# CLASS AL6 / 86

| | |
|---|---|
| **Original Numbers:** E3101-E3200 | |
| **Built:** August 1965 to October 1966 | |
| **Number built:** 100 | |
| **Contracted to:** English Electric Vulcan Foundry / BR Doncaster | |
| **Weight:** 81 tons | |
| **Continuous rating hp:** 3,600 — English Electric; 4,000 BR Doncaster | |
| **Max speed:** 100mph, 110mph for Class 86/1 | |
| **Withdrawn:** Still in service with Freightliner, and on the main line in preservation. Some have been exported | |

The knowledge and experience gained from Class AL1 to AL5 was used to advantage in the development of the second generation of AC locomotives. They were initially Class AL6 and during the classes career, which in December 2012 is still on-going, has produced sub-classes namely 86/1, 86/2, 86/3, 86/4, 86/5, 86/6, 86/7 and eventually 86/9. Many locomotives were modified during their careers to become members of several different sub-classes.

The order for 100 locomotives was placed in 1963, with BR Doncaster and English Electric Vulcan Foundry. The first of the class was built at Doncaster; No E3101 (later 86252) entered service in August 1965.

The 'AL6s' had features shared with the 'AL5s' as far as body superstructure, suspension and bogies. The 'AL6s' were 2ft longer than the 'AL5s' and had smaller wheels thus allowing a much better internal layout. Unlike the

other prototypes the traction motors were axle-hung. Once the class was in daily service and operating at high speed, it became apparent that the high unsprung weight of the traction motors was resulting in a poor ride quality at speed and also causing bogie frames to crack, plus causing track damage.

Locomotive No E3173 (later 86204) was selected to be fitted with helical spring suspension (known as flexicoil). Another 57 members of the class were modified and became Class 86/2. Four of the Class 86/2s were altered for 110mph running and fitted with Brecknell-Willis designed pantographs, replacing the standard Stone-Faveley type, becoming Class 86/1s.

As mentioned earlier, there were many sub-classes to the Class 86 (AL6) where modifications were carried out to suit specific purposes, and details will be provided in the captions that follow.

The class has proved a terrific investment for the railways, as after 47 years the class can still be seen in revenue service hauling freightliners, with others being available for spot hire, plus those that have been exported for further use.

*Below:* No E3167 is shown between Rugby and Nuneaton on a down express in 1968. It entered service in August 1965 and was renumbered 86228 in December 1973. It was named *Vulcan Heritage* between March 1980 and October 2003 when it was eventually stored at Long Marston. *Mike Mensing*

*Left:* The 12.45 Holyhead–Euston heading south near Polesworth with No E3196 (later No 86219) in charge on 18 August 1968. It received the name *Phoenix* at Willesden on 6 August 1979. It was stored in November 1995, and the nameplates remained attached until October 2001, after which it was moved by road to Immingham where it was cut up in May 2002 by Easco. *Mike Mensing*

*Right:* No E3123 (later Nos 86015, 86315, 86415, 86615) and named *Rotary International* in June 1984 makes a fine sight at the head of the 4.15pm Euston–Birmingham–Manchester Piccadilly, east of Marston Green between Coventry and Birmingham in 1968. The locomotive was cut up at Rotherham in July 2007. *Mike Mensing*

*Left:* On 24 August 1968 an up empty stock working is passing Easenhall north of Rugby headed by No E3192 (later No 86201 and 86101) which was named *Sir William A. Stanier FRS* between October 1978 and December 2001. It passed into preservation and can occasionally be seen working on the network. *Mike Mensing*

*Above:* The 3.25 pm Liverpool Lime Street–Birmingham–Euston is shown east of Marston Green on the Birmingham–Coventry line headed by No E3120 (later renumbered 86019, 86319 and finally 86419) being named *Poste-Haste — 150 Years of Travelling Post Offices* on 13 July 1990. It was stored at Crewe in March 1999 and withdrawn on 18 October 2002, before being cut up by Sandbach Car & Commercial Dismantlers Ltd in March 2003. *Mike Mensing*

*Below:* A fine picture of No E3174 (later No 86022, 86322, 86422 and finally 86622) passing Adderley Park on the Coventry line out of Birmingham New Street. It is heading an up Liverpool Lime Street–Euston in July 1968, and is still at work with Freightliner. *Mike Mensing*

*Left:* Class 86 No 86007 passes the coal yard just to the north of Rugby station on 16 June 1979 with a down express. Originally numbered E3176, it then carried the following numbers — 86007 July 1973, 86407 May 1987 and finally 86607 in August 1988. It was also named *Institution of Electrical Engineers* between July 1987 and March 1997. Currently it can still be seen on the WCML hauling freightliners after 47 years of service. *Gavin Morrison*

*Right:* A cross-country service changes over from Class 47 haulage (No 47284) to Class 86/2 at the west end of Birmingham New Street on 25 August 1980. No 86249 was originally built as No E3161, becoming 86249 in April 1974, and retained this identity until withdrawn in November 2002. It was used at Polmadie depot for driver training, and was still there in January 2004 and was named *County of Merseyside* on 7 September 1981. It was one of 58 members of the class to be modified as '86/2', which included the fitting of flexicoil suspension units and new resilient wheels. Gear ratios were raised, which produced much better riding qualities and less track damage. *Gavin Morrison*

*Left:* The 13.00 Euston–Blackpool passes the carriage sheds to the south of Crewe and approaches the station headed by Class 86/3 No 86325 on 22 October 1983. The locomotive was originally No E3186, became 86025 in November 1973, 86325 in April 1980 and finally 86425 in February 1986, until withdrawn in December 2002. They became Class 86/3s when fitted with SAB resilient wheels, which allowed them to be operated at 100mph. They were also fitted with jumper cables for multiple working. These were cheap alternatives to a full conversion to Class 86/2 and it did little to reduce track damage. BR therefore decided in 1984 to fit the Class 86/3s and remaining Class 86/0s with flexicoil suspension units, which gave an additional 38 100mph locomotives. *Gavin Morrison*

AC ELECTRIC LOCOMOTIVES in colour

*Right:* The 8.10 from Penzance to Liverpool Lime Street is arriving at Wolverhampton station on 17 June 1978. It is headed by No 86038 which was originally No E3108, but later became Nos 86438 and 86638 for Freightliner, where it is still working in 2012. In the background is No 86252, the first of the class and originally numbered E3101. It carried two names, *Liverpool Daily Post* from November 1980 to July 2000, and then *Sheppard 100* from August 2000 until withdrawn in February 2002 by Anglia. *Mike Mensing*

*Below:* The up 'Manchester Pullman' left Piccadilly for Euston at 4.43pm. It is shown on 14 May 1979 just south of Lichfield Trent Valley station headed by No 86206, which was originally number E3184, and named *City of Stoke on Trent* between December 1978 and October 2002. It was finally taken off-lease on 1 November 2002 and eventually got to Alstom at Springburn, Glasgow, for overhaul. Instead it was earmarked for conversion to a mobile Load bank locomotive for Network Rail, but conversion never took place. After a period at MoD Pig Bay, Shoeburyness, it went to Sims Metals, Cardiff, for scrap, in February 2004. *Mike Mensing*

*Below:* A lengthy van train heads south through Carlisle station headed by Class 86 No 86019 and Class 83 No 83001 on 17 May 1980. No 86019 was the second-built Class AL6 as No E3102. It became 86009 in October 1973, was modified and renumbered 86409 in November 1986 and finally became 86609 in June 1989. In 2012 it is still in service with Freightliner. *Gavin Morrison*

*Left:* The up 'Manchester Pullman' in InterCity livery leaves Manchester Piccadilly with Class 86/2 No 86228 *Vulcan Heritage*, on 8 June 1984. It received the name at Warrington Bank Quay station on 29 March 1980. It is currently (2012) stored at MoD Long Marston having been withdrawn in June 2003. It was part of Virgin Cross-Country fleet and received the Virgin colours around October 2000, but in January 2001 it was surprisingly repainted into InterCity livery, which it retained until withdrawn. *Gavin Morrison*

*Right:* Due to the previous night's serious crash at Nuneaton, a down Euston express finds itself diverted via Coventry and Bescot and is approaching Aston station on the Stetchfield line on 6 June 1995. No 86247 is in charge (originally numbered E3192) and carried the name *Abraham Derby* between October 1981 and October 2003 when it came off lease, arriving at Immingham Reception sidings in November and then moving to the Railfreight terminal. It was moved to Long Marston and became a demonstrator locomotive for Europhoenix, a company that has bought over 20 Class 86s to refurbish for export. *Mike Mensing*

*Below:* Class 86 No 86003 is shown on freight duties, passing Moore, south of Warrington, on 2 September 1981 whilst restricted to 80mph as a Class 86/0. Built at Doncaster as No E3115, it became 86003 in May 1973. It was modified to Class 86/4 as No 86403 in June 1986 and then to a 75mph locomotive as a '86/6' in November 1990. Prior to its conversion to a Class 86/4, it was involved in an accident and was out of use from 13 August 1985 till June 1986. It was withdrawn in October 1995 and eventually sent to Wigan Springs Branch to be stripped for spares. *Gavin Morrison*

*Left:* Seen on 29 July 1978 before it was named *City of Chester* on 7 March 1979 No 86207 (originally No E3715) is heading the 11.18am Birmingham New Street–Euston and has just emerged from Beechwood tunnel, west of Tile Hill on the Birmingham–Coventry line. The nameplates were removed in May 2003, but it had been taken off lease on 12 July 2002. After several moves it was stored at MoD Longtown on 4 December 2002. It was eventually cut up by Ron Hull Junior at Rotherham in April 2006. *Mike Mensing*

*Below:* Class 86/2 No 86254 races through Acton Bridge with an up express on 24 March 1983. It entered service as No E3142 and became 86047 in January 1974. It was allocated No 86254 in December 1974 and was named *William Webb Ellis* at Euston station on 9 October 1980. In its later years it was allocated to RES (Rail Express Services), but spent a lot of time in store between 1995 and 2002, when it was withdrawn. *Gavin Morrison*

*Above:* On 14 June 1986 Class 86/1 No 86103 appears to have only recently received its InterCity livery. Named *Andre Chapelon* on 21 January 1981 it is at Liverpool Lime Street after working an express from Euston. Originally No E3143 it ran as No 86203 for a period after September 1972, but was selected in July 1974 along with numbers E3150 and E3191 for further modifications, and had new BPG bogies and Brecknell-Willis high speed pantographs fitted which allowed the maximum speed to be increased from 100mph to 110. The three locomotives in this form became the Class 86/1s and were really the test beds for the 36 Class 87s which had been ordered for the WCML extension to Glasgow. Note the offset quartz headlight which was fitted to two of the three Class 86/1s. It was taken out of service in May 1995 and was used as a source of spares for other locomotives, eventually ending its days at Immingham Railfreight terminal where it had been cut-up by November 2002. *Gavin Morrison*

*Right:* This view inside Crewe Works on 20 July 1990 shows Class 86/1 No 86102 being moved around the maintenance shop. Originally No E3150, it became No 86202 in December 1972 and then 86102 in July 1974, after the modifications already described in the previous picture. It was named *Robert A. Riddles* at Euston station on 19 May 1981. Stored in May 1995, it moved to many different locations until August 2001, when it was unexpectedly hired to Freightliner along with No 86101 in August 2001, but the following month it was hired to Virgin Trains for Thunderbird duties. This only lasted until April 2002 when it finished up stored at MoD Longtown. It was eventually broken up at Caerwent, South Wales, in early 2005. *Gavin Morrison*

*Left:* A familiar sight at Euston station for any years. On 25 March 1994. Class 86/2 No 86248 is ready to depart with a down express; Class 87 No 87001 *Royal Scot* can be seen in the background. It was built at Doncaster as No E3107 and was allocated No 86248 in April 1974. It received the name *County of Clwyd — Sir Clwyd* at Crewe station on 19 March 1981, and was taken off lease on 1 November 2002. After storage at several sites it arrived at Long Marston MoD, from where it was refurbished and sold to Hungary. *Gavin Morrison*

*Right:* From 1981, British Railways slowly extended the electrification out of Liverpool Street until it ran through to Norwich by 1985. A dedicated batch of Class 86s was out-based at Ilford for the services; eventually they were maintained at Norwich Crown Point depot. In InterCity days No 86232 (originally E3113) passes Witham station with the 11.00 Norwich–Liverpool Street on 10 June 1989. It carried three names during its career; *Harold Macmillan* from October 1979 to September 1990, followed by *Norwich Festival* between October 1990 and October 1995 and finally *Norwich and Norfolk Festival* from October 1995 to July 2005, when it was stored at MoD Long Marston. Class 312 EMU No 312794 on the right is on the 12.31 slow service from Witham to Liverpool Street. *Mike Mensing*

*Left:* A view taken from a passing train on 6 September 1988 sees a selection of Class 86s and others at Willesden depot. The depot was built as a dedicated depot for AC locomotives when electrification reached London Euston. *Martin Welch*

*Above:* In 1988 it was decided that Freightliner needed a dedicated fleet of Class 86s, so InterCity lost eight Class 86/2s which were re-geared for 75mph and had multiple jumper cables fitted. This arrangement was short-lived as by the summer of 1989 they were returned to InterCity and their Class 86/2 condition. Freightliner received eight Class 86/4s from InterCity instead. A very clean No 86507 was named *L. S. Lowry* on 6 October 1980. Originally No E3169, it became 86239 in February 1974, 86507 in February 1989 and was back to 86239 in July 1989. It became part of the RES fleet, but its career ended dramatically when working the 21.40 Travelling Post Office train from Coventry to Glasgow at 23.08 on 8 March 1996. It hit some derailed wagons at Riverscote, south of Stafford, at speed with such force that the locomotive was spun round and the force of hitting other wagons sent the locomotive up the embankment, landing a few feet from a house. It was withdrawn on 30 April 1996 and scrapped at MRJ Phillips around May 1997. It is seen here at Beckfoot on 13 May 1989. *Gavin Morrison*

*Below:* The 150th anniversary of the railway link between Scotland and England via the Caledonian route was in February 1998. Virgin Trains decided to celebrate the occasion by painting No 86245 into this one-off blue livery and naming it *Caledonian*, at a ceremony at Glasgow Central on 15 February. It ran in this livery until October 2003. It was named *Dudley Castle* between August 1984 and January 1998. The picture was taken at Preston on 4 July 1998, when it was working the 9.05 1Z48 Birmingham–Glasgow. *M. Langton*

*Left:* A very rare occasion, possibly the only visit of Class 86/2 to Leeds, was when No 86234 *J. B. Priestly O.M.* hauled an InterCity special from London King's Cross to Carlisle as far as Leeds. Originally numbered E3155, it became 86234 in January 1974. Whilst working for Anglia it received the odd name of *Suffolk — Relax — Refresh — Return* on 7 February 2004. It continued in service with Anglia until the arrival of the Class 90s and was withdrawn in April 2005 and sent to Long Marston for storage. The HST on the left was about to leave Leeds City for King's Cross on 18 February 1989. *Gavin Morrison*

*Right:* In the latter 1980s and early 1990s Stratford Works in London was giving major overhauls to the AC electric locomotives. On 12 February 1989 No 86437, which had just received a 'G' exam, is alongside Class 87 No 87005. It received several numbers during its career starting with No E3130 before becoming 86037 in May 1974, 86437 followed in May 1986 and finally 86637 in November 1990. It is one of the few members of the class never to carry a name, and is still currently (December 2012) working for Freightliner Intermodel. *Gavin Morrison*

*Left:* Heading south through the fine scenery of the Clyde Valley on 23 September 1992 is the 15.55 Edinburgh Waverley–Paddington headed by Class 86/2 No 86236. Originally numbered E3133 it became 86236 in February 1974. It was named, appropriately, at Wedgwood halt near Stoke on Trent *Josiah Wedgwood Master Potter 1730-1795* on 6 November 1980. It came off lease on 1 November 2002 and was sent to MoD Longtown for storage. Eventually in August 2003 it was dragged to Immingham where it was scrapped by Easco on 1 December 2003. *Gavin Morrison*

*Left:* Recently ex-works in the first InterCity livery, Class 86/2 No 86220 approaches Nuneaton station with a set of coaches still in the old BR livery on 3 April 1986. It was one of the last Class 86s to be built at English Electric Vulcan Foundry, entering service in July 1966 as No E3156. It received No 86520 in November 1973 and was named *Goliath* at Willesden on 8 August 1978. After it moved to Anglia it was renamed at Norwich station *The Round Tabler* on 5 May 1987. It was taken off lease on 10 May 2002 and after storage at MoD Longtown, was sent to Immingham where it was scrapped by Easco on 28 November 2003. *Gavin Morrison*

*Right:* Allocated to RES (Rail Express Services), No 86210 is parked up inside Norwich station awaiting an evening working to the capital on 3 April 1986. It began its career numbered E3190, becoming 86210 in August 1973. The name *City of Edinburgh* was applied on 27 February 1979, this being the fourth choice of name, and the locomotive was renamed *C.I.T. 150th Anniversary* at Manchester Piccadilly on 13 December 1994. It was in and out of store several times between February 2000 and was withdrawn in January 2004. It became one of the two Class 86/2 to be converted to Class 86/9s for Network Rail for load bank testing, along with No E3136 (86044, 86253). *Gavin Morrison*

*Above:* Class 86s were introduced on the Great Eastern services out of Liverpool Street to Ipswich in 1985 and Norwich in 1987. Originally an InterCity service, it became part of Anglia, followed by ONE, and is currently Greater Anglia. The Class 86/2s were replaced by Class 90s after 17 September 2005 when No 86235 ran between the two cities for the last time. Originally E3194, it became No 86235 in January 1974. Named *Novelty* in June 1980, this was followed by *Harold Macmillan* in October 1990 and finally *Crown Point* after the Norwich depot on 27 October 1992. It is seen here on 19 August 1989 climbing Bethnal Green bank, just out of Liverpool Street, heading the 11.30 to Norwich. No 86235 is currently (2012) stored at MoD Long Marston. Gavin Morrison

AC ELECTRIC LOCOMOTIVES in colour

Left: To mark the Queen's Golden Jubilee in 2002 the Union Jack flag was applied to selected locomotives by some companies. Anglia selected Class 86/2 No 86227 and named it *Golden Jubilee* at Ipswich station on 17 July 2002. The locomotive started its career as No E3117 and was then allocated No 86227 in December 1973. It received the name *Sir Henry Johnson* which it carried between March 1981 and April 2002. Withdrawn in October 2004, it was scrapped at Ron Hull Junior, Rotherham in July 2005. It is seen crossing the River Stour, approaching Manningtree station at 11.55, with an up express on 21 February 2003. *Gavin Morrison*

Above: The 10.40 Norwich–Liverpool Street is running 20 minutes late on 24 August 2004 as it passes Forest Gate station with No 86221 (originally No E3132), which carried the name *BBC Look East* between 11 May 1987 and May 2003. It was taken out of service, eventually ending up at Immingham Railfreight Terminal where it was scrapped by Easco in November 2003. It also carried the name *Vesta* between 25 May 1979 and April 1987. *Mike Mensing*

Above: In the distinctive Anglia livery, No 86246 (originally numbered E3149) is propelling the 11.30 Liverpool Street–Norwich service past Stratford station on 24 August 2000 . It received the name *Royal Anglian Regiment* at Liverpool Street station on 13 March 1985, retaining it until January 1988. It then carried the name *Pride of the Nation* between 15 January and December 1988, but it was refitted again in March 2001. It was converted to an 86/5 and renumbered 86505 between October 1988 and September 1989. It was stored at Long Marston in December 2004 where it survives in 2012. *Gavin Morrison*

Above: On 14 July 1998 two Class 86/2s stand by the buffer stops at Liverpool Street station. No 86218 has just been repainted into the Anglia livery. The locomotive will propel the train back to Norwich with Mk 2 coaches and a Mk 2 DBSO (originally used on Scottish Region services) at the front. *Gavin Morrison*

*Above:* On 4 September 2001 the 15.30 Manchester Piccadilly–Birmingham New Street is arriving at Stockport station hauled by Class 86/2 No 86256 *Pebble Mill*, a name it received at Birmingham International station on 17 November 1981. The plates were removed in April 1993 and refitted again a month later. It was taken off lease on 1 November 2002 and cut up at Ron Hull Junior's at Rotherham in May 2006. Its original number was E3135, changed to 86040 in November 1973 and finally No 86236 in March 1975. *Gavin Morrison*

*Below:* No 86233, originally E3172 when it entered service in June 1964, was selected by Virgin Trains in 2002 to be repainted into the original Electric Blue livery. The work was carried out at Alstom's Willesden depot. It was presented to the railway media on 24 June 2002, named *Crewe Heritage*, complete with cast numbers and the lion emblem. Together with the red-liveried Virgin coaches it presented a fine sight. It was normally used on Euston–Birmingham services, where it is seen in this picture at Brockhall near Weedon heading for Euston on 8 April 2003. It also carried the name *Laurence Olivier* between June 1980 and May 2002 and was withdrawn in October 2003 and stored for possible future use. *Gavin Morrison*

*Left:* After working a freight from the north into the yards at Ipswich, two of Freightliner's Class 86/6s, Nos 86610 and 86632, are heading for the locomotive stabling yard at the side of the station on 21 February 2003. Both locomotives are still currently (2012) active in the Freightliner fleet. No 86610 was released into traffic in October 1965 as No E3104, 86010 followed in July 1973, and after modification it became No 86410 in August 1986, finally becoming No 86610 in July 1990. No 86632 was new as No E3148 in April 1966, then became No 86032 in March 1974, followed by 86432 in January 1985, eventually becoming No 86632 in August 1989. *Gavin Morrison*

*Right:* The 14.06 1V64 Low Fell–Plymouth, seen on 4 July 2001, was regularly hauled by RES and EWS Class 86s around this period. Class 90s were also frequently seen, the electric worked the train as far as Doncaster. No 86401, an EWS locomotive is shown south of Gateforth at bridge 12 on the Selby diversion. It was originally numbered E3199, then 86001 in May 1973 and finally 86405 in December 1986. It carried the name *Northampton Town* between May 1989 and October 1991 and was unique in being the only member of the class to carry Network SouthEast livery which it received in January 1987 to celebrate completion of the Cambridge electrification project. In October 1998 to December 2002 it carried the name *Hertfordshire Rail Tours*. It was withdrawn in December 2002 and is now preserved by the AC Locomotive Group in NSE colours and is currently operational but not main line certified. *Gavin Morrison*

*Left:* The RES and EWS Class 86s were frequently used by Virgin Trains for their express services. Here No 86210, then named *C.I.T. 75th Anniversary,* propels the 17.27 Manchester Piccadilly–Euston out of Stockport on 27 July 2002. The locomotive became No 86902, and its history details are given on page 36. *Gavin Morrison*

*Right:* On 23 July 2004 Class 86/2 No 86230, in Anglia livery, is at the rear of the 15.46 on arrival at Stowmarket from Liverpool Street. It was new in June 1965 as No E3168 and became No 86230 in January 1974. It was named *The Duke of Wellington* at Euston on 11 June 1981, carrying the name until April 1997. It was withdrawn in October 2001 and was sent to MoD Long Marston. *Gavin Morrison*

*Above:* The unique Class 86/5 No 86501 is heading north near Weaver junction at the head of the 4M81 Felixstowe–Ditton freightliner at 17.59 on 8 June 2006. The locomotive is unique within the Class 86s and has carried many different numbers during its career. Starting with No E3180 when new in October 1965, 86008 followed in June 1973, 86408 in November 1985, 86608 in September 1989 and finally 86501 in May 2000. It has also carried two different names, *St John Ambulance* from November 1987 to September 1999 and then unofficially *Crewe Basford Hall* for three days, 19-21 May 2000. Freightliner, back in 2000, intended to give major overhauls to its fleet of Class 86s, and No 86501 was selected to have its tractive effort increased by 31.5%, making it capable of doing the work of double-headed Class 86/6s. Its maximum speed was 75mph and improvements were made to its rail adhesion. The modifications were a success, but a change of mind by management resulted in no more conversions. No 86501 is still (2012) in traffic despite catching fire in 2008. *Gavin Morrison*

*Below:* Class 86/2 No 86247, named *Abraham Derby* between October 1981 and October 2003, heads the 8.10 Virgin express from Euston to Liverpool Lime Street. It is seen just about to enter Linslade tunnel to the north of Leighton Buzzard on 24 June 2003. It was originally No E3192 when new in December 1965 and became No 86247 in April 1974. It was withdrawn in October 2003 and sent to MoD Long Marston where it still resides in 2012. *Gavin Morrison*

*Above:* A very clean No 86258 *Talyllyn — The First Preserved Railway*, the name carried between April 1984 and May 2001, is ready to depart Glasgow Central with the 8.40 to Penzance on 17 May 2001. It had many different numbers, starting with No E3140 in March 1966; 86046 followed in March 1974, 86258 until becoming 86501 in May 1975 for a short period before returning to 86258 in November 1989. It was a Virgin Cross-Country locomotive and lasted until July 2002, and was sent to Long Marston. It carried a variation to the name shown, *Talyllyn — 50 Years of Preservation 1951-2001,* between May 2001 and July 2002, and also *Ben Nevis* in December 1995. *Gavin Morrison*

*Right:* The nameplate carried by No 86258. *Gavin Morrison*

*Left:* A couple of Freightliners Class 86/6s, Nos 86609 and 86632, head south on the 10.14 Trafford Park Manchester–Ipswich freightliner, passing South Kenton at around 15.10pm on 8 June 2005. No 86609 has had a similar history to other Freightliner Class 86/6s. Starting as No E3102 in August 1965, it became 86009 on October 1973, then 86409 in November 1986 and finally 86609 in June 1989. The history of No 86632 is given on page 39; both are still in service in 2012. *Gavin Morrison*

*Above:* Class 86/2 No 86233 became a celebrity locomotive in the Virgin fleet after a superb restoration job at Willesden depot in June 2002. A ceremony on 24 June 2002 saw it named *Alstom Heritage*, complete with 'lion' emblem, silver cast numbers and original livery. It was selected to work the last Virgin Class 86-hauled passenger train, the 1A19 7.19 Wolverhampton–Euston on 24 June 2003, and it was taken off lease on 2 October 2003. It had several identities after starting with E3172; 86233 followed in January 1974, and it became one of the short-lived Class 86/5s, No 86506, until it reverted to 86233 in July 1989. It is shown heading the 15.15 Euston–Birmingham New Street at Brockhall near Weedon on 8 April 2003. *Gavin Morrison*

*Left:* Nameplate from No 86233. *Gavin Morrison*

*Right:* Three Freightliner grey-liveried locomotives at the front of a down freightliner pass Forest Gate station in east London on 24 August 2000. Class 90144 was dead in the train, the other two Class 86/6s were Nos 86610 and 86623. No 86610 was originally No E3104 and became No 86010 in July 1973, then 86410 in August 1986 and 86610 in July 1990. No 86623 started as No E3152, then 86023 in December 1973, 86323 in August 1880, 86423 in November 1986 and finally 86623 in December 1990. It was withdrawn in 2010. *Mike Mensing*

*Above:* 1M74, the 13.41 Coatbridge–Crewe Basford Hall freightliner, negotiates the curves near Thrimby Grange headed by Class 86/6s Nos 86632 and 86639 on 10 July 2008. The picture was taken from the A6 road bridge at Shapbeck. The history of No 86632 was given on page 39, whilst No 86639 started its career in May 1966 as No E3153. In October 1974 it became 86039, then in October 1986 to 86439 and finally 86639 in December 1990. Both locomotives are still active at the end of 2012 with Freightliner on the West Coast main line. *Gavin Morrison*

*Below:* Seen on 24 January 2006 the two Network Rail Class 86/9s, Nos 86902 named *Rail Vehicle Engineering* and No 86901 *Chief Engineer* are inside York station on platform 1 where they had been based during the winter months for overhead power line ice-scraping. No 86901 was E3190, whilst No 86902 was originally No E3136 when new in December 1965. It became 86044 in February 1974 and then 86253 in January 1975 before being converted to an '86/9' in December 2004. Both were converted to mobile load bank locomotives at Barrow Hill, and their primary use is to test the 25kV AC overhead power supply. They can run under their own power but cannot haul any significant weight. *Gavin Morrison*

*Above:* As of December 2012 two of the Freightliner Class 86/6s, Nos 86622 and 86637, have received this latest livery. No 86622 is at Coatbridge depot awaiting its next duty on 2 November 2011. *Gavin Morrison*

*Right:* Europhoenix-owned Class 86/7 No 86701 has just received the Colas livery as part of the freight operator's plan to work a night-time service from Daventry to Euston for supermarkets using ex First Great Western Motorail Vans. It is seen at Milton Keynes at the head of a trial run from Rugby on 24 October 2012 with Class 56 No 56087 at the rear. No 86701 was taken into stock in November 1965 as No E3129. It became No 86205 and was named *City of Lancaster* at Lancaster station on 25 October 1979. It was taken off lease in April 1998, eventually ending up at Immingham from where it was purchased and refurbished by Europhoenix. *Andrew Chambers*

*Left:* On 14 June 2012 Class 86/2 No 86259 *Les Ross* in the attractive electric blue livery heads the Railway Touring Company's 'Cumbrian Mountain Express', 1Z86 Euston-Carlisle, past Old Linslade, which it worked as far as Carnforth. Steam then took over for a trip on the Settle–Carlisle. It entered service in January 1966 numbered E3137, becoming 86045, followed by 86259. It received the name *Peter Pan* in October 1979 but was renamed *Greater Manchester The Life & Soul of Britain* in October 1995. The present name followed in April 2002. It was taken off lease in October 2003 and in October 2003 stored at Immingham Freightliner Terminals, eventually to be restored to working order. *Andrew Chambers*

# CLASS 87

| | |
|---|---|
| **Original Numbers:** 87001-87035 and 87101 | |
| **Built:** June 1973 to March 1975 | |
| **Number built:** 36 (including '87/1') | |
| **Built by:** BREL Construction, Crewe, GEC main electrical parts and design work | |
| **Weight:** 83.3 tonnes | |
| **Continuous rated hp:** 5,000 | |
| **Max speed:** 110mph | |
| **Withdrawn:** From November 2004. Last passenger working for Virgin Trains, 10 June 2005. 21 exported to Bulgaria | |

With the sanctioning of electrification through to Glasgow, the BRB realised that it would need more locomotives with greater power than the Class 86s. An order was placed for 36 locomotives, capable of 110mph running. They were fitted with GEC412AZ traction motors to give a better ride, which were frame mounted and 'flexicoil' suspension. The front-end design was different from the previous classes, there being only two windows, no reporting number panel and a single GEC cross-arm pantograph. They were air-braked only, plus they had multiple-unit working. In their early years they were diagrammed for freight work as well as passenger.

With the experience gained from the previous classes, and in particular the three modified Class 86/1s, after a few initial problems, the class settled down and gave around 30 years of trouble-free service with maintenance being provided by Willesden depot. The locomotives had little notice taken of them in the magazines and seldom hit the headlines. They enjoyed an almost serious-accident-free existence, except for No 87027's crash with a 'Pacer' unit at Winsford North junction on 23 June 1979. Only in the last few years of operation, when a few members received one-off liveries did they receive a following. They lasted until June 2005 on passenger work for Virgin Trains, and a few continued on a very limited basis working Royal Mail trains. Most were stored at Long Marston and 17 were refurbished and exported to Bulgaria.

*Below:* No 87017 named *Iron Duke* at Willesden TMD on 30 May 1978, prepares to leave Coventry station at 13.07 with an up express from Birmingham New Street to Euston on 12 September 2003. It is in the Virgin livery, having carried BR blue, InterCity and Virgin colours during its 30-year career, which started in 1974 and ended when it came off lease in January 2004. It is now working in Bulgaria. *Gavin Morrison*

*Left:* Carrying the name *City of Glasgow* which it received eight months before, No 87006 is arriving at Stoke-on-Trent on the 15.55 from Euston to Manchester Piccadilly on 12 August 1978. It was unique in carrying a large-logo grey livery in 1984, prior to the introduction of InterCity colours. It was also the first of the class to receive the Virgin colours. After its days with Virgin were over it joined the DRS fleet and was painted blue, and after withdrawal it ended up at MoD Long Marston, and is now working in Bulgaria. *Mike Mensing*

*Right:* No 87022 entered service in April 1974. It ran nameless for four years until receiving the name *Cock o' the North* in June 1978, a famous name from the steam era. This name was replaced by *Lew Adams — The Black Prince* at Preston station on 2 October 1998. The locomotive passed to GBRF and was painted in a blue livery after it finished work with Virgin Trains. It was the last of the class to work on Network Rail before being stored at MoD Long Marston, refurbished and exported to Bulgaria in BR blue livery. It is shown heading a down express rounding the sharp curves on the WCML at Weedon on 9 September 1978. *Gavin Morrison*

*Above:* The Scottish lowland scenery of the upper Clyde valley is seen to advantage in this picture of No 87002 (named *Royal Sovereign* at Willesden on 4 July 1978) as it heads towards Beattock summit, just south of Crawford, on the 17.20 Edinburgh Waverley–Birmingham New Street on 4 May 1980. It suffered fire damage near Coventry on 8 October 1998 and was repaired at Willesden. Its period of fame was in 2003, when it was painted in a purple Porterbrook livery, which it retained until it came off lease. Along with No 87010 it hauled the last Class 87 working for Virgin Trains on 10 June 2005. It is now preserved by the AC Locomotive Group and is occasionally seen on Network Rail. *Gavin Morrison*

         *AC ELECTRIC LOCOMOTIVES in colour*

*Above:* Back in the days when the Class 87s were regularly working freightliners and other freights, No 87029 makes a colourful sight as it heads south past Crewe with an up freightliner working on 1 June 1985. It was named *Earl Marischal* at Willesden TMD on 26 June 1978, and after its days with Virgin Trains ended it was withdrawn in November 2004, to be stored at MoD Long Marston before being exported to Bulgaria. *Gavin Morrison*

*Below:* The openness of the landscape back in 1974 near Shap summit is shown in this picture of No 87003 when it was just a year old, heading a down express of 11 coaches on the approach to Shap summit on 20 July 1974. The 5,000hp available will hardly have noticed the 1 in 75 gradient. It received the name *Patriot*, also used by the famous LMS class, on 13 June 1978. After withdrawal in 2005, it went to MoD Long Marston and is now in Bulgaria. *Gavin Morrison*

*Right:* During the latter 1970s No 87004 was often selected for Royal Train duties. Heading a Silver Jubilee tour to Lancashire, it is passing Outbeck loops, just south of Lancaster, on a down trip to Carnforth to turn after the Queen and the Duke of Edinburgh had got off at Preston. It then worked the train for the up journey on 20 June 1977. No 87004 did not receive the name *Britannia* until 3 April 1978, again a name used by BR for one of its Standard class locomotives. Its days with Virgin Trains ended in 2005, and like most of the class it went to MoD Long Marston. It is currently working in Bulgaria. *Martin Welch*

*Left:* No 87025 approaches Watford station with a down express, when it carried the InterCity 125 livery with yellow roof panel, on 9 July 1991. It was named *County of Cheshire* at the time, having received the name at Crewe station on 29 November 1982. It was previously named *Borderer* between 26 April 1974 and October 1982. It continued in service with Virgin Trains until December 2004, then moved to Long Marston for storage. It was exported to Bulgaria in November 2012. *Gavin Morrison*

*Above:* The nameplate from No 87025. *Gavin Morrison*

*Left:* Although the up liner train is headed by Class 86/4 *County of Lancashire*, I have included it in the Class 87 section to give another illustration of Class 87s at work on freight services. No 87012 was named *The Royal Bank of Scotland* on 10 November 1988, the plates being removed in February 1998. In May 1978 it was named *Coeur de Lion* which it carried until July 1988 when one plate was stolen, the other was soon removed. It was renamed *Coeur de Lion* in January 2001. In its latter years it was painted in a Network SouthEast livery advertising the 2012 Olympics which it retained until withdrawn in 2006. After a stay at MoD Long Marston, it became one of the first '87s' to go to Bulgaria, still in its NSE livery. It is seen at Beckfoot on 13 May 1989. *Gavin Morrison*

*Left:* Plenty of power available for this up freight leaving the yard just north of Bletchley station on 20 March 1990. It is headed by No 87029 *Earl Marischal* double-heading with Class 90 No 90034. History details of No 87029 are given on page 47. It is painted in InterCity 125 livery with yellow cab roof. *Gavin Morrison*

*Right:* On 25 August 2000 the empty stock for the 17.00 Glasgow Central–Euston approaches Central station hauled by Class 87 No 87018 *Lord Nelson* in InterCity swallow livery. It received its name at Liverpool Lime Street station on 9 March 1978. It was taken off lease in January 2004 by Virgin Trains and sent to Long Marston and scrapped. *Gavin Morrison*

*Left:* No 87006 *City of Glasgow* received this experimental livery of dark grey with large BR logo and numbers. It was compared with the InterCity livery applied to No 87012 *Coeur de Lion*, which became the standard InterCity livery. The grey livery was short lived, this picture being taken of it in Crewe works on 2 June 1984. The locomotive is now at work in Buglaria. *P. Corrie*

*Right:* No 87030 *Black Douglas* approaches Stafford station with the 1F18 13.15 Euston–Liverpool Lime Street on 30 June 2001. It was named at Willesden on 10 July 1978. It came off lease in 2005, was stored at MoD Long Marston and scrapped. *Gavin Morrison*

*Below:* On a superb winter's day in the Shap Fells, 4 January 2003, the 10.30 Euston–Glasgow ('Royal Scot') heads up the 1 in 75 gradient past Greenholme Scotchmans Bridge, headed by No 87004 *Britannia*, whose details are given on page 48. *Gavin Morrison*

*Right:* The 9.10 Euston–Liverpool Lime Street is coming off the 49-span Ditton viaduct at the north end of Runcorn viaduct over the River Mersey and Manchester Ship Canal on 14 January 2003. It is headed by No 87014, named *Knight of the Thistle* at Willesden on 12 May 1978. Its career with Virgin Trains ended in 2005 before it was moved to Long Marston and then exported to Bulgaria. *Gavin Morrison*

*Above:* The Euston–Glasgow Central express was running late on 30 August 2003. It was believed that the train locomotive, No 87019 *Winston Churchill*, had failed at Preston and that No 87024 *Lord of the Isles* had come to the rescue. The train is at Beckfoot before passing Low Gill and into the Lune gorge. No 87019 was named at Willesden on 3 May 1978, whilst No 87024 received its name three weeks later at Willesden. No 87019 is now at work in Bulgaria, whilst No 87024 was not so fortunate and was scrapped in 2005. *Gavin Morrison*

*Below:* Birmingham International is the setting for this picture of No 87015 *Howard of Effingham* propelling a Birmingham New Street–Euston express into the station at 12.55 on 26 February 2003. It was named on 12 May 1978 and remained in service with Virgin Trains until November 2004. It was cut up in 2005. *Gavin Morrison*

*Right:* The 8.30 from Euston has arrived at Glasgow Central on 19 May 2002 behind No 87027 *Wolf of Badenoch* with DVT (Driving Van Trailer) No 82136 at the wrong end of the train and the wrong way round. There was another DVT at the other end. No 87027 was the only member of the class to receive serious accident damage, when it was hauling the 1S47 6.30 Euston–Glasgow on 23 June 1999 and ran into the rear of two Class 142 Pacer units (Nos 142008 and 142003) at Winsford South junction. The Class 87 demolished the rear carriage of Pacer unit No 142008 which was withdrawn. No 87027 was sent to Crewe and was repaired and back in traffic towards the end of August 2000. It then continued in service with Virgin Trains until August 2004, when it was taken off lease and finished up at Long Marston, to be used as a source of spares for the locomotives going to Bulgaria. It was extremely fortunate that the Pacer units were empty at the time, otherwise the incident would have been far more serious. Considering the millions of miles clocked up by the class over the years, only one serious accident is an excellent record, but nevertheless one too many. *Gavin Morrison*

*Top:* A rare working for a Class 87, seldom seen on the East Coast main line, occurred on 18 April 2006 when No 87002 hauled 1S04, the 16.05 Willesden–Shieldmuir via the East Coast route. The train comprised Class 325 Royal Mail units Nos 325012, 325007 and 325013. Unfortunately, by the time it arrived at Colton junction, just south of York, it was nearly dark. No 87002 was named *Royal Sovereign* in July 1978, which it carried until being renamed *AC Locomotive Group* in 2005. In its latter days it became a celebrity locomotive when it was painted in the distinctive Porterbrook livery. It is now part of the AC Locomotive Group and certified for main-line running. *Gavin Morrison*

*Above:* After 31 years of service, the first Class 87 No 87001 is seen at the rear of an up Euston express at the north end of Crewe station on 6 June 2004. It was originally named *Stephenson* in January 1976, but only carried the name until July 1977, when it became *Royal Scot*. The name Stephenson was in connection with the Stephenson Locomotive Society (SLS). After removal the plates were transferred to Class 87/1 No 87101. It became *Stephenson* again in 2003 when it was repainted in BR blue by Virgin Trains, becoming *Royal Scot* again when it passed into preservation at the National Railway Museum. *Gavin Morrison*

*Above:* The nameplate and plaque on No 87002. *Gavin Morrison*

*Top right:* After Virgin Trains had finished with members of the class, four were taken up by Direct Rail Services (DRS), Nos 87006/22/28/32. This was because the Strategic Rail Authority at the time issued a directive that freights working north of Preston must have electric traction. Three of the four were painted into this blue livery, with No 87032 missing out and not entering service. Nos 87006/22/28 entered service with DRS in November 2004 on Mossend–Daventry workings. It soon became clear that this was uneconomic, as the trains originated at Grangemouth and had to be diesel-hauled to and from Mossend, so the Class 87s were taken off and the working went diesel. This left the three operational '87s' with little work, other than helping out with Royal Mail workings and occasional specials. No 87006, unnamed and without decals is passing Doncaster Black Carr, heading the short-lived 'Blue Pullman' on 14 April 2006, which it took to Edinburgh, and the return working, the train going to Inverness and Thurso. No 87006 carried the names *City of Glasgow* from December 1977 to March 1987, then *Glasgow Garden Festival* from April 1987 to about November 1988, and finally *George Reynolds* on 21 November 1997. All three ceremonies took place at Glasgow Central station. No 87006 is now at work in Bulgaria. *Gavin Morrison*

*Bottom right:* As mentioned in the previous caption, No 87022 became part of the DRS fleet in November 2004. Here, on 7 June 2006, it makes a very colourful sight passing Red Bank near Warrington hauling two Royal Mail Class 325s on 1M44, the 15.47 Shieldmuir to Warrington. Note the 'First' decal on the front. Details are given on page 46. The locomotive was exported to Bulgaria in 2008. *Gavin Morrison*

*Above:* Looking immaculate in its purple Porterbrook livery, No 87002 *Royal Sovereign* passes Ashton, north of Milton Keynes, propelling an up Euston express for Virgin Trains on 14 June 2003. Locomotive details are on pages 52 and 46. *Gavin Morrison*

*Above:* No 87012 was painted in a version of Network SouthEast livery by its owners Porterbrook in February 2005. It was named *The Olympian* on the 25th of the month at Euston station, and carried the message 'Back the Bid London 2012' in white on its side. After four months in service in the livery for Virgin Trains, it could be seen from mid-2005 appearing occasionally hauling Royal Mail Class 325 EMUs. Here, on 8 June 2005, it is seen passing Carpenders Park on the 18.22 Euston–Northampton express, these workings to and from Northampton being known as the 'cobblers' by the commuters. Further details are for No 87012 are on page 48. *Gavin Morrison*

*Below:* No 87019 was the recipient of another one-off livery for the class. This time it was London & North Western lined black livery, and it was named *Association of Community Rail Partnership* at Crewe station on 15 March 2005. It carried a green-backed nameplate on one side and a blue on the other. Here, on 8 June 2005, it is propelling the 16.40 Euston–Wolverhampton past Headstone Lane during its short period with Virgin Trains in this livery. It was one of the first of the class to be exported to Bulgaria. Further details on it are on page 51. *Gavin Morrison*

*Left:* On a fine mid-summer's morning I was surprised at the number of people, about four, who visited the graveyard at Old Linslade Church, and who were more than a little surprised to see me standing on an aluminium ladder waiting to photograph the trains between 7 and 8 am on 8 June 2005. My reason for being there was to get the 'Caledonian Sleeper' and No 87012 working the Northampton–Euston commuter 'cobbler' service. Details of No 87012 have already been given on pages 48 and 54. *Gavin Morrison*

*Right:* The nameplate of No 87010. *Gavin Morrison*

*Below:* Virgin Trains rose to the occasion to commemorate its last electric locomotive-hauled service by Class 87s on 10 June 2005. The train was the 9.38 from Euston to Manchester Piccadilly, hauled by No 87010 *Driver Tommy Farr* and Porterbrook-liveried No 87002 *The AC Locomotive Group*. Both locomotives were very well turned out and were greeted at Manchester by a large gathering. They took the empty stock back to Longsight and so ended an era of 32 years on the West Coast services. Details of No 87002 have already appeared on pages 45, 52 and 53. No 87010 carried the name *King Arthur* from June until April 2005 when it received the name *Driver Tommy Farr*, and is now at work in Bulgaria. *Gavin Morrison*

The final member of the Class 87s was to have been No 87036 but it was decided to fit it with experimental features, the main one being 'thyristor' control, plus better anti-slip protection. It was introduced in March 1975, but it was not until January 1977 that it entered revenue service. This was due to extensive testing by Derby Research Department. It has been reported that it was at the time the best AC electric locomotive on BR, and had about a 20% better hauling ability than a Class 87/0. It received the name *Stephenson* on 12 October 1977, as recognition of the Stephenson Locomotive Society (SLS). Being a one-off it was transferred to Railfreight in April 1989. It was in an accident in March 1991 at Lichfield Trent Valley station, but was returned to service, although it had been stored for most of 1989 and early 1990. After repair it emerged from Crewe in Freightliner livery. It was stored again for the first nine months of 1995. Its last working was on 18 January 1999 on the 4S90 2.48 Willesden–Mossend as far as Basford Hall. It was scrapped in February 2002 by Harry Needle at Barrow Hill.

*Above:* On 26 July 1982 No 87101 is at the south end of Springs Branch depot awaiting its next duty. *The Stephenson* nameplate, which it received at Manchester Piccadilly on 12 October 1977, can clearly be seen together with the Coat of Arms. *Gavin Morrison*

*Left:* On a dull Sunday in January No 87101 is ready to leave Liverpool Lime Street on the 16.00 to Euston, although by this date, 20 January 1990, the locomotive had been allocated to the Railfreight sector and it had moved from Willesden to Crewe ETD for maintenance. *Gavin Morrison*

*Right:* No 87101 *Stephenson* was involved in an accident at Lichfield in March 1991, after which it emerged from Crewe Works repainted in the Railfreight grey livery. It had its ETH equipment isolated, and was limited to 75mph. It ventured onto the Freightliner services to Harwich during 1994, then had another visit to the works and reappeared in BR blue livery. It became part of the Railfreight DAMC pool and operated with the Class 90s. It is on display at a Crewe Basford hall open day on 21 August 1994. *Gavin Morrison*

# CLASS 89

**Numbered:** 89001

**Built:** 1986

**Number built:** 1

**Constructed by:** Designed by Brush, constructed at BREL Crewe

**Weight:** 105 tons

**Continuous rated hp:** 5,830

**Max speed:** 125mph

**Withdrawn:** 1991 (second time)

With the authorisation to electrify the East Coast main line in 1984, BR InterCity issued a specification for a suitable locomotive, which resulted in Brush Traction being awarded the contract to supply what became the Class 89. It was constructed at BREL Crewe over a period of two years, and emerged on 2 October 1986 and was taken to Brush at Loughborough for the fitting of six TM-2201A traction motors. It returned to Brush in March 1987 and was sent to the Railway Technical Centre at Derby for extensive testing. Its first powered working was on 9 February 1987, and on the 20th it had its first sole outing on the main line. It returned to Derby RTC and thence to the Old Dalby test track until May 1987, when more trials took place over Shap and Beattock. It arrived at Hornsey on 9 December 1987 and its first run on the ECML was on 21 December. Its next six months were occupied by being sent to an International Railway Exhibition at Hamburg. Upon its return it started services between King's Cross and Peterborough. On 15 July 1985 it received the name *Avocet* on 16 January 1989.

It was technically a far more advanced locomotive than the previous classes, with a Co-Co wheel layout, compared to all the others which were Bo-Bos. This provided better downward track forces and higher outputs, making it the most powerful electric locomotive to be built in the UK, until the arrival of the Class 91s. However BR policy changed when fixed-formation trains were decided upon for ECML workings, with Class 91 locomotives and Mk 4 stock, so the Class 89, in spite of its performance being a success, had no useful purpose to perform.

As the Class 91s entered service the '89' had less and less work and was withdrawn on 30 July 1992. It was preserved and kept fit for service by a group of Brush Traction employees at its new home at Butterley.

Surprisingly in September 1996 it was bought by Sea Containers, the parent company of GNER, to cover for Class 91s away for overhaul. After overhaul at Brush it re-entered service in 1997 and was frequently seen working between King's Cross and Leeds. It performed well until 1999 when it developed a series of faults that proved expensive for GNER. In July 2001 GNER management decided to remove it from main line duties and use it as a static train shore supply unit at Bounds Green depot. This duty ceased in December 2002, and eventually it returned to preservation at Barrow Hill, where it currently resides.

*Below:* After its overhaul at Brush in 1997, No 89001 returned to main-line duties for GNER mainly between King's Cross and Leeds. On 19 July 1997 it is shown at Leeds City resplendent in its GNER livery with white lettering, but nameless. It is at the rear of the 11.05 to King's Cross. It was during this period between April 1997 and August 1998 that the locomotive was in regular use, and covered the greater part of its mileage. *Gavin Morrison*

*Left:* On 3 July 1998, to commemorate the 50th anniversary of Sir Nigel Gresley's Class A4 No 4468 *Mallard* capturing the world speed record for steam of 126mph, a special train was run from King's Cross to Scarborough, hauled from King's Cross to Doncaster and return by the Class 89 *Avocet*. Unfortunately, back in 1988 the southern end of the ECML was out of bounds to steam, so *Mallard* took over at Doncaster for the journey to Scarborough, witnessed by a huge crowd of people. Little attention was paid to the Class 89 on this occasion, but it is shown approaching Bridge junction to the south of Doncaster station. It is in the InterCity 125 livery, at the head of 11 very smart InterCity coaches. *Gavin Morrison*

*Right:* Sometime during the latter half of 1988 during one of its frequent works visits, *Avocet* received the InterCity swallow livery, which it is carrying on 21 January 1989, as it enters Leeds City at the head of a 14-coach special from King's Cross to Carlisle via the Settle & Carlisle line. The train went forward behind Class 45/1 'Peak' No 45106, which was painted for a short period at this time into the old plain BR green colours. *Gavin Morrison*

*Left:* During its 16-month period of being mainly used on the King's Cross–Leeds–Bradford Forster Square workings (April 2007 to August 2008), No 89001 is approaching Shipley on 4 September 1997 with the 11.36 from Bradford Forster Square to King's Cross. It often appeared on this diagram. *Gavin Morrison*

AC ELECTRIC LOCOMOTIVES in colour

# CLASS 90

| | |
|---|---|
| **Numbered:** 90001-90050 | |
| **Built:** 1987-1990 | |
| **Number built:** 50 | |
| **Constructed by:** BREL Crewe, GEC for electrical equipment | |
| **Weight:** 84½ tons | |
| **Continuous rated hp:** 5,000 | |
| **Max speed:** 100mph | |
| **Withdrawn:** None as at 2012 | |

The Class 90s were the last locomotives to be ordered by British Rail before sectorisation. Authorisation by the government was given in 1985. Initially it was envisaged the class would just be an update of the Class 87s, so they were allocated Class 87/2. As it became clear there was little resemblance in looks and many technical aspects, they were reclassified as '90'.

They were far more attractive-looking locomotives than the previous designs, with the raked-back cab ends. They were fitted with Time Division Multiplex (TDM) multiple working gear, and thyristor controls. Four G-412CY traction motors were supplied by GEC for each locomotive, and electric rheostatic and air brakes were fitted. A single Brecknell-Willis high-speed pantograph was used and a pneumatically-operated sanding gear fitted to give better adhesion. Another first was the fitting of drop-head buckeye coupling gear.

No 90001's first public appearance was at a Crewe open day in July 1987, but the locomotive was not complete. It went to the Railway Technical Centre at Derby in September 1987. Delivery of other locomotives proceeded slowly, as BREL Crewe was under pressure to complete Class 91s for the ECML. No 90050 was not released until September 1990. After extensive testing and trials, No 90005 was the first of the class to haul a revenue earning service in March 1988.

With the experience gained over the last 30 years, and with similarities to the Class 87s, no doubt BR expected trouble-free operation for the class. Unfortunately this was not the case and after a year only three or four could be found working at the same time. Faulty relays were sorted out by GEC and all those in service on 16 August 1989 were taken out of traffic to have safety checks on the brakes, but then they settled down and are still giving excellent service. InterCity received the first 15 members of the class, painted in the swallow livery and the next 11 were Mainline-liveried to show they were for mixed-traffic duties;, in reality they spent nearly all their time on InterCity trains. The final 14 (Nos 90037-50) went to Railfreight Distribution (RfD) and were painted grey. At Sectorisation in 1991 the class was redistributed as follows: InterCity 90001-15, Parcels 90016-20, Railfreight Distribution 90021-50. As all locomotives were to the same specification, InterCity continued to borrow locomotives, until RfD decided to isolate the ETH, reduce maximum speed to 75mph and to fit high-phosphorous brakes and remove the buckeye couplings from 25 of their

fleet (Nos 90026-50), they were reclassified as '90/1'.

In 1992, three locomotives (Nos 90128/129/130) received liveries of the Belgian, German and French railways, and No 90136 received a special RfD variation.

No 90021-24 kept their original '90/0' specification and were frequently hired out for East and West Coast passenger duties. The Parcels, later Rail Express Systems (RES) locomotives were also frequently seen on passenger work. At privatisation the RfD fleet was split, 10 of the locomotives, Nos 90141-50, being transferred to Freightliner, the remainder of the RfD passing to English Welsh & Scottish (EWS) as well as the RES locomotives. The 15 InterCity locomotives were taken over by Virgin Trains.

EWS gained the ScotRail sleeper services from Virgin in 1988, and to add to its five Class 90/0s, it converted Nos 90125-29 back to Class 90/0s. In due course EWS converted all its Class 90/1s back to '90/0' specification. Nine EWS locomotives became Class 90/2s for a short period before reverting back to Class 90/0 numbers.

In August 2004 Virgin Trains finished with its fleet of the original InterCity locomotives (Nos 90001-15) as the Pendolinos took over, and they were sent to 'one Anglia' where they currently (2012) remain on the London–Norwich services. The Freightliner locomotives are still hard at work, except for 90050 which has been out of service since 2004, and has been replaced by EWS (now DBS) No 90016. The rest of the EWS (DBS) fleet currently has little work, except for the ScotRail sleepers, resulting in many being in store in 2012.

These fine locomotives will be around for some time yet, and have over the years been painted in a wider variation of colourful liveries than probably any other class.

*Above:* The last Class 90, No 90050, is shown nearing completion at BREL Crewe on 13 August 1990. To the left is No 90049, which was fully painted and almost ready for despatch, and in the background is a Class 91 under construction. *Gavin Morrison*

*Left:* On 13 May 1989 No 90016 in full InterCity swallow livery negotiates the curves at Beckfoot, near Low Gill, with the 8.30 Glasgow Central–Euston, before the introduction of Driving Van Trailers (DVTs). It received RES livery and is now working for Freightliner in their green livery. *Gavin Morrison*

*Right:* No 90005 was the first of the class to be accepted into BR stock, the class entering revenue-earning service during 1988. It received the name *Financial Times* at Euston on 30 March 1988, but the plates were removed in September 1997. It is at the buffer stops at Manchester Piccadilly after arriving with the 12.00 service from Euston on 11 May 2000. It is currently (2012) working on the Liverpool Street–Norwich services. *Gavin Morrison*

*Left:* No 90010 in InterCity swallow livery appears to have lost its nameplate *257 Railway Squadron (Volunteers)* which it received at Euston on 15 November 1989. It is in the up main line platform at Stafford, hauling a track recording special from Glasgow to Euston, with test car DB999508 at the rear on 8 April 1992. In 2012 it is working on the Liverpool Street–Norwich services. *Martin Welch*

*Right:* Although it is in full InterCity livery, No 90022 was originally one of the nine locomotives allocated to mixed traffic duties, which is well demonstrated here by it being shown approaching Watford in the afternoon of 9 July 2001 on a Felixstowe–Mossend freightliner. It was displayed at the National Exhibition Centre (NEC) where it was named *Freightconnection* on 3 September 1992. It was renumbered 90222 in 2001, but reverted to 90022 in 2002. Now part of the DB Schenker fleet, but in EWS livery, it is currently stored. *Gavin Morrison*

*Left:* A trio of Class 90s, Nos 90032, 90040 and 90031, plus an unidentified Class 86 are seen at the locomotive stabling point alongside Ipswich station awaiting their next duties on 1 June 1991. All of them became Class 90/1s in July/August 1991, reverting to Class 90/0s in June/July 1999. No 90032 is in Mainline livery and was named *Cerestar* on 2 June 1994, No 90040 *The Railway Mission* on 11 October 2001 and No 90031 *Intercontainer* in February 1997 until July 2000, when the name was replaced by *The Railway Children Partnership — Working for Street Children Worldwide* at the Old Oak Common open day on 5 August 2000. All locomotives are now in EWS livery, in store. *Gavin Morrison*

*Right:* Mainline-liveried No 90029 on InterCity duty enters Macclesfield at the head of the 17.30 Manchester Piccadilly–Euston on 10 May 1989. In August 1991 it was painted into DB (German railways) red livery, named *Frachtverbindungen* and became No 90129; see page 66. It is currently in EWS livery. *Martin Welch*

*Above:* In dramatic winter sunlight, on 20 January 2003, Virgin-liveried No 90009 *The Economist* propels the 13.40 Glasgow Central–Euston across the River Lune at Lancaster. It was named *Royal Show* between 25 May 1989 and March 1994. It was named *Diamond Jubilee* on 30 April 2012, with a Union Jack painted on the side by Greater East Anglia. *Gavin Morrison*

*Right:* The 16.00 Willesden–Shieldmuir vans head north past Weedon Wharf, headed by No 90027 *Allerton T&RS Depot Quality Approved* on 7 April 2003. It carried No 90127 from 10 July 1991, then 90027 again, followed by 90227 on 2 February 2001 and back to 90027 from 18 June 2002. It is in the first RfD livery, and was the last of the class to retain it. It is currently (2012) stored. *Gavin Morrison*

*Left:* No 90002 *Mission Impossible* was the first of the Class 90s to receive the Virgin livery. It is seen passing Brockhall, just north of Weedon, on 8 April 2003. It was named *The Girls Brigade* on 6 April 1993, but the name was altered to *Mission Impossible* on 10 March 1997. It had a very protracted entry into service, entering BR stock on 4 April 1988. It was used for testing, was taken out of service for rectification, then spent time at Ilford depot for driver training, and then donated parts to other locomotives whilst at Crewe Works. It eventually started regular service on 25 November 1989 and in 2012 was still working for Greater Anglia. *Gavin Morrison*

*Above:* The original management team at Virgin Trains thought fit to allow advertising on a few locomotives. Here No 90014 advertises the 'Big Dish' at Euston before heading north with an express on 24 September 1998. Fortunately this practice was short-lived, and the adverts were removed, and in the case of No 90014 lasted from 26 June 1998 to November 1999. On 16 June 2002 it was renamed *Driver Tom Clark OBE*, after the driver of the non-stop record runs between London and Glasgow in 1936, with Stanier Pacific No 6201 *Princess Elizabeth*. It also carried the name *The Liverpool Post* between 21 March 1990 and April 1997. The locomotive is currently part of the Greater Anglia fleet working the Liverpool Street–Norwich services. *Gavin Morrison*

*Below:* Two of the Freightliner fleet of ten Class 90s, Nos 90044 and 90050, both in the grey livery, head north past Rugby on the afternoon of 24 September 2003 with an Ipswich–Trafford Park freightliner. Both received the Class 90/1 numbers 90144 and 90150 in July 1991 before going back to 90044 and 90050. No 90044 is still hard at work, but No 90050 has been out of traffic since 2004, and has been exchanged with DB Schenker's No 90016. *Gavin Morrison*

*Left:* Taken during the period between 16 July and August 2002, when it was renumbered 90141, Freightliner's Class 90 passes through Stratford station with a freightliner heading for Ipswich, while a Class 321 prepares to leave for Liverpool Street on 14 July 1998. It reverted to No 90041 in August 2002 and is currently still working for Freightliner in their green livery. *Gavin Morrison*

*Right:* The 4M74, the afternoon Coatbridge–Basford Hall Crewe freightliner headed by No 90047, is passing Brock, between Preston and Lancaster, at 17.41 on 25 April 2005. It ran as No 90147 and retained the number for longer than any others, because whilst hauling the 4L60 15.00 Coatbridge–Ipswich freightliner on 18 March 2002 it caught fire near Shap and serious damage was caused. It was sent to Crewe where parts were removed to get No 90044 back in traffic. It is now back in service. *Gavin Morrison*

*Left:* Class 90 No 90041 and Class 86/4 No 86426 are seen in the stabling point for locomotives at the side of Ipswich station on the evening of 21 March 2003. Details of 90041 are given above whilst Class 86/4 No 86426 was on long-term hire to Freightliner from EWS, and had been repainted into the Freightliner green livery, but was withdrawn and cut up at C. F. Booth, Rotherham, in November 2005. *Gavin Morrison*

*Right:* No 90130 was named *Fretconnection* in September 1992, and was repainted into SNCF (French railways colours), which was officially unveiled at the exhibition at the NEC between 3 and 5 September 1992. It was numbered 90130 in July 1991, and back to 90030 in June 1990. Repainted into EWS livery in March 2000, it received the name *Crewe Locomotive Works* at the open weekend on 20 May 2000. Now part of the DB Schenker fleet, it was photographed at Crewe ETD on 15 October 1994 but is currently stored. *Gavin Morrison*

*Left:* No 90028 in the SNCB livery (Belgian railway colours) that it received in September 1992 when named *Vrachter-Binding*. It was numbered 90128 between July 1991 and March 1998, when it reverted to a Class 90/0 so it could be hired out for passenger work, as seen here when it is propelling the 12.40 Leeds City–King's Cross past Sandal & Agbrigg on 24 September 1999. It is now in DB livery in the DB Schenker fleet. *Gavin Morrison*

*Right:* No 90129 was the third Class 90 to receive a continental railway livery, this one being the DB (German) red. Named *Frachtverbindungen* when repainted in September 1952, it also attended the NEC exhibition. It was renumbered back to 90029 in March 1998, and is shown in this picture at the east end of Edinburgh Waverley station after working an overnight sleeper from Euston on 25 October 2001. It is currently in the DB Schenker red livery. Class 47/7 No 47744 is also in the bay platform. *Gavin Morrison*

*Above:* Recently repainted in the Freightliner green livery, No 90041 passes South Kenton at the head of the 10.24 Felixstowe–Trafford Park freightliner at 15.40 on 8 June 2005. Historical details of No 90041 are given on page 64. *Gavin Morrison*

*Below:* Another picture of 90044 in Freightliner grey livery, passing Shap Summit at 16.56 on 6 September 2005 hauling the 4M74 14.10 Coatbridge–Basford Hall service. *Gavin Morrison*

*Above:* The 4M81 09.00 Felixstowe–Ditton freightliner passes Great Brington at 14.19 on its way north on 7 June 2005. Historical details of No 90016 are on page 60, but it is slightly different from the other two green-liveried Class 90s (Nos 90041 and 90046), in that the Freightliner name is placed a little lower than on the others. *Gavin Morrison*

*Below:* The 16.00 Liverpool Street–Norwich heads past Dunston near the end of its journey on 9 September 2006, propelled by the unique Railfreight/EWS liveried No 90036, hired in by 'one' from EWS to help out with a motive power shortage. *Gavin Morrison*

*Right:* The 15.36 Glasgow Central–Euston has just arrived at Carlisle, with Virgin liveried No 90011 *West Coast Rail 250* at the rear on 2 May 2002. It received this name on 12 April 2000, but on 10 October 1988 it was renamed *The Chartered Institute of Transport* which it carried till March 2000. It is currently on Greater Anglia services between Liverpool Street and Norwich. *Gavin Morrison*

*Left:* On a wet night of 22 December 2002 No 90006 *Roger Ford/Modern Railways Magazine* (different plates on each side of the locomotive) has just arrived with the 14.28 Glasgow Central–Euston. The separate plates were affixed on 26 June 2001; it had previously carried the name *High Sheriff* from 1 May 1992 to 23 June 2001. One of the original InterCity Class 90s, it is now with Greater Anglia. *Gavin Morrison*

*Right:* A view inside Polmadie depot at Glasgow on 12 August 1999. No 90029 *Frachtverbindungen* and No 90027 *Allerton T&RS Depot Quality Approved* had both worked the previous night's sleepers from Euston and would return in the late evening. Details of 90029 appear on pages 61 and 65, whilst No 90027's are on page 62. *Gavin Morrison*

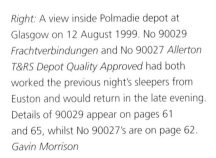

*Right:* The 3.30am mail from Wembley was running nine hours late on 31 January 2003 with a very unusual combination of power consisting of Class 90 No 90026 in EWS livery, No 90019 in RES livery, plus one Class 325 unit and 'Royal' Class 47/7 No 47798 *Prince William*. The train is heading north past Chelmscote near Leighton Buzzard. No 90026 was renumbered to 90126 In July 1991 until March 1998. It carried the name *Crewe Electric Depot Quality Approved* from 10 March 1993 until 14 October 1994, when it became *Crewe International Electric Maintenance Depot* from 15 October 1994 until November 2002. No 90019 was named *Penny Black* on 1 May 1990 until February 1997. No 90019 is now in First Scotrail livery. *Gavin Morrison*

*Left:* On 27 October 2001 the 10.10 King's Cross–Leeds has Freightliner No 90142 in charge. It was on hire to GNER and had obviously been modified to provide heat and run at 110mph. Nos 90142 and 90147 were frequently hired out for passenger work around this period. It is shown at Carcraft near Doncaster. *Gavin Morrison*

*Right:* The 16.24 Willesden–Shieldmuir is passing South Kenton, hauled by RES-liveried No 90017 on 15 July 2002. It was named *Rail Express Systems* (one plate) and *Quality Assured* (second plate) on 8 March 1995. The names had been removed by the date of this picture. It is currently in EWS livery (2012) and stored. *Gavin Morrison*

*Right:* Freightliner's No 90043 is on hire to Anglia Railways. It is seen on 21 February 2003 propelling the 9.30 Liverpool Street–Norwich over the River Stour at Manningtree North Junction. It carried the number 90143 between July 1991 and August 2002. *Gavin Morrison*

*Left:* A rare working for a Class 90 on the East Coast main line. No 90034 in EWS livery is at the head of the 6E28 14.00 Wembley–Tyne Yard on 30 June 2004. It is approaching Colton junction to the south of York. It was numbered 90134 from August 1991 to June 1999. The locomotive is currently stored (2012). *Gavin Morrison*

*Right:* The sheep pay little attention to the Virgin Class 90 crossing North Roade viaduct, south of Macclesfield, with a Euston–Manchester Piccadilly express on 27 July 2002. *Gavin Morrison*

*Above:* One of Freightliner's fleet of Class 90s, No 90150, heads a down train past Manor Park station in east London at 11.28am on 20 July 2001. This locomotive has been stored unserviceable since 2004 and is now owned by DB Schenker who exchanged it for one of their own Class 90s, No 90016. *Mike Mensing*

*Below:* The pioneer Class 90, No 90001, named *BBC Midland Today* when in service with Virgin Trains has now lost its name since joining Greater Anglia. On 25 August 2006 it is seen passing Trowse, near Norwich, at 13.30, heading for Liverpool Street. *Gavin Morrison*

*Right:* Heading up the East Coast main line at Burn on the Selby diversion is EWS Class 90 No 90028 *Vrachtverbinding* in its special Belgium livery with the 14.46 Low Fell–London mail, which consists of two Class 325 EMUs on 23 February 2001. *Gavin Morrison*

*Left:* One of the three First Scotrail-liveried Class 90s No 90019 is inside Edinburgh Waverley station on 8 September 2007 after working the previous night's sleeper (16 coaches) from Euston. It was originally part of the InterCity fleet, then passed to Rail Express Systems named *Penny Black* with a Penny Black badge and repainted in the RES red livery; it is now in First Scotrail livery for working the sleeper services. *Gavin Morrison*

*Right:* Class 90 No 90024 has never carried a name, but was unique in being the only member of the class to receive the old GNER livery, as back in 1988 EWS signed a deal to provide a Class 90 for at least a year to work on their King's Cross services. To celebrate the contract No 90024 received the livery in May 1999 from the Toton paintshops. It retained the livery long after its duties on the ECML, where in practice it was seldom seen, and currently carries the First Scotrail livery. Minus the GNER lettering, it is entering Euston with the empty stock for the 21.05 sleeper to Fort William, Inverness and Aberdeen on 6 July 2004. *Gavin Morrison*

*Right:* An immaculate EWS Class 90, No 90032, named *Cerestar* on 2 June 1994 but now nameless enters Carlisle at 7.56am on 2 May 2002 with the very lightly loaded 2.50am Willesden–Mossend 4S99 intermodal. This was a member of the class to be converted back from a '90/1' to a '90/0' in July 1999, but is currently stored (2012).*Gavin Morrison*

*Left:* In 1994 ScotRail had to hand back the Class 322 EMUs being used on the North Berwick services to Stansted Express. The most unlikely replacement for the services was Class 90s working in push/pull mode with ex-Virgin DVTs and coaches. Part of the plan was to provide work during the day for the '90' working the sleeper services, although additional locomotives were needed. Here, on 15 September 2004, No 90026 is arriving at North Berwick; the old single-road steam shed used to be directly behind the locomotive. *Gavin Morrison*

*Right:* No 90040 *The Railway Mission*, named on 11 October 2001, rounds the curve off the single-track North Berwick branch to join the East Coast main line at Drem junction. It is heading the 12.17 from North Berwick to Edinburgh Waverley on 15 September 2004. The locomotive is now stored (2012). *Gavin Morrison*

*Right:* Taken from the A120 road bridge at Stowmarket, Class 90 No 90006, in the first version (darker blue) of the 'one Anglia' livery, leaves at 16.31 on 28 July 2004 for Liverpool Street. In InterCity days the locomotive was named *High Sheriff* from 1 May 1992, unusually at York station, and then on 21 June 2001 *Roger Ford* on one side and *Modern Railways Magazine* on the other. *Gavin Morrison*

*Left:* Before all fifteen ex-Virgin Trains Class 90s could be repainted into 'one' livery after their transfer to the Norwich–Liverpool Street services they ran without the Virgin decals, but in the red/black livery. Here No 90005 in this condition arrives at Diss at 17.16 heading for Liverpool Street on 28 July 2004. *Gavin Morrison*

*Right:* Unnamed No 90011, in the second version of the 'one' livery, catches the evening light at Dunston, a few miles south of Norwich, as it heads the up 17.30 Norwich–Liverpool Street service on 9 September 2003. It currently carries the unusual name *Let's Go East of England*. *Gavin Morrison*

*Right:* It is easy in the summer months to photograph the Scotrail 'Caledonian' sleepers at the south end of the West Coast main line, and in the north of Scotland. On a glorious 29 June 2003 morning the up Fort William/Inverness/Aberdeen (portions combine at Edinburgh Waverley) passes Ledburn junction, just south of Leighton Buzzard, headed by Class 90 No 90031, named *The Railway Children Partnership — Working for Street Children Worldwide* which it received at the Old Oak Common open day on 5 August 2000. No 90031 is now stored (2012). *Gavin Morrison*

*Left:* At this location, Cathiron/Little Lawford, it is seldom possible to photograph the up sleepers unless they are running very late. This was the case on this date, when the empty stock was passing the location just north of Rugby in the early afternoon after failing to complete its journey the previous night due to problems around Stafford. No 90034 presented a fine and unexpected sight on 5 May 2006. No 90034 is now stored (2012). *Gavin Morrison*

*Right:* It is 7.05 on a lovely summer's morning, 8 June 2005, as No 90027 *Allerton T&RS Depot Quality Approved* (named on 10 March 1993) passes Old Linslade, just north of Leighton Buzzard, with the up Edinburgh/Glasgow sleeper that had left the cities just after midnight. No 90027, although currently stored, was the last of the class to retain the old Railfreight Distribution livery with EWS stickers. *Gavin Morrison*

*Left:* No 90024, still in GNER livery (see page 72) but without branding is shown propelling an up Virgin Trains express past Soulbury, between Bletchley and Leighton Buzzard, at 13.00 on 6 January 2003. It is currently (2012) in First Scotrail livery. *Gavin Morrison*

*Right:* Three Class 90s, Nos 90019, 90021 and 90024, have received the First Scotrail livery for working the 'Caledonian' sleeper services. Here No 90021 is shown at Chelmscote heading the 13.14 Euston–Crewe service on Sunday 4 November 2007. *J. Turner*

*Left:* No 90008 is shown at Dunston heading the 1P53 17.30 Norwich–Liverpool Street service on 30 May 2009. *P. Corrie*

*Right:* No 91025, seen under construction at Crewe on 13 August 1990, was taken into stock at Bounds Green on 17 October. It was named *BBC Radio One FM* at King's Cross on 30 September 1992, carrying the name until December 1996. It became *Berwick-upon-Tweed* on one side only on 25 July 2000. The major overhaul was completed on 13 January when it became 91125 with the name on both sides. *Gavin Morrison*

*Left:* On 13 August 1990 No 91023 was almost complete at Crewe; it was taken into stock on 18 September 1990. This was destined to be the most famous, or infamous, Class 91 for all the wrong reasons, as it was the locomotive involved in both the disastrous accidents at Hatfield on 17 October 2000 and Heck on 28 February 2001. The opportunity was taken to renumber it as No 91132, leaving 91123 blank. Fortunately it has continued in service since 2001 named *City of Durham* without further mishaps. It is currently running nameless. *Gavin Morrison*

*Right:* No 91003, on driver training, is about to leave Leeds City with a rake of Mk 1 coaches for the south. Generally the class is very seldom seen working blunt end first. It had been in BR stock six months when this picture was taken on 12 October 1988. No 91003, together with Class 89 No 89001 and Class 90 No 90008, was sent to an international exhibition in Hamburg held between 1 and 12 June 1988. It didn't receive the name *The Scotsman* until 25 February 1993, which it carried until February 1997. Outshopped after refurbishment on 30 August 2001, it carried the name *County of Lincolnshire*, and was renumbered 91103 on 4 September 2001. It is currently running nameless. *Gavin Morrison*

*Right:* After being serviced at Neville Hill depot, Leeds, No 91031 propels the empty stock into Marsh Lane cutting *en route* to Leeds City on 28 April 1991. It was the last of the class and was handed over to BR on 11 February 1991, and was named *Sir Henry Royce* at Crewe on 7 June 1991. On 2 June 1995 it attained a speed of 154mph with a passenger service, for which it carries a plaque. It was renamed *County of Northumberland* on 4 April 2000. With its refurbishment completed on 16 October 2002, it became 91131. *Gavin Morrison*

*Left and below:* On 30 April 1992 the London Midland Region hired Class 91 No 91029, with five coaches and a DVT from the Eastern Region. It was for a high-speed outing from Euston to Manchester Piccadilly and return, for the invited press and Olympic 2000 guests. No 91029 is seen at Platform 5 at Piccadilly and leaving on the return. The locomotive entered BR stock on 23 January 2001 and was named *Queen Elizabeth II* at King's Cross on 28 June 1991. Its refurbishment was completed on 4 October 2002. *M. Welch*

*Right:* A distant view of No 91016 passing Moorthorpe junction between Doncaster and Wakefield Westgate with a down King's Cross–Leeds express on 19 September 1991. The Swinton & Knottingley line can be seen in the background. No 91016 did not receive the name *Strathclyde* until it was released from refurbishment on 11 December 2001. *Gavin Morrison*

*Left:* The 7.50am King's Cross–Bradford is passing Wortley Junction South near Leeds on 10 April 1997. It is headed by No 91028, still in InterCity livery, with the then new GNER colours. No 91028 entered BR stock on 17 January 1991, and was named *Guide Dog* at King's Cross on 24 July 1991, carrying this until April 1997 when it was renamed *Peterborough Cathedral* on 14 May 1999. Its refurbishment was completed on 28 December 2001. *Gavin Morrison*

*Right:* No 91025 negotiates the complicated track layout on the approach to Glasgow Central with the 11.00 service from King's Cross on 11 June 1992. It entered stock with BR on 17 October 1990, but remained unnamed until 5 November 1990. Further details of the locomotive are on page 81. *Gavin Morrison*

*Above:* For a short period at the start of the GNER franchise, the company had white lettering on the locomotives, but soon moved onto the gold colour. No 91001 is shown in this livery heading the 14.30 King's Cross–York past Bridge junction, just south of Doncaster station, on 10 April 1992. It was the first member of the class and was handed over on 14 February 1988. It received the name *Swallow* on 20 September 1989, which it carried until January 1997. Refurbishment was completed on 15 May 2001, and it was re-named *City of London* on 14 October 2002. It is currently unamed. *Gavin Morrison*

*Below:* A picture of No 91023 before its involvement in the disastrous Hatfield and Heck accidents. It is shown passing Bishops Wood on the Selby diversion, racing north at 125mph, at the head of the 17.30 King's Cross–Edinburgh service on 15 July 1996. Its history details are given on page 81. *Gavin Morrison*

*Above:* No 91019 is at Newcastle on the 9.00 King's Cross–Edinburgh service on 21 January 1997. Note the red-coloured name instead of the normal gold. It was named *Scottish Enterprise* on 12 September 1990 and was the first '91' to work into the Scottish capital. The name was removed in October 1996 and *County of Tyne & Wear* was carried after refurbishment was completed on 4 November 2002. It originally entered BR stock on 8 August 1990. On the left is HST No 43160 ready to depart with a cross-country service. *Gavin Morrison*

*Below:* No 91009 *The Samaritans* (note red name) is working the wrong way round as it propels the 16.05 Leeds–King's Cross past Bentley on the outskirts of Doncaster on 18 August 1998. Initially the locomotive seems to have been used for testing, four days of which were on the West Coast main line (24-27 April 1989) and does not appear to have been taken into stock until around July 1989. Named *Saint Nicholas* on 5 December 1992 until March 1996, it then received the Samaritans name on 9 April 1997, which became *The Samaritans* in January 2002. Refurbishment was completed on 10 August 2001. *Gavin Morrison*

*Right:* The North Sea can be seen in the background as No 91124 *Reverend W. Awdry* heads south as it approaches Alnmouth on 17 March 2004. It was the last of the class to be refurbished, being outshopped on 8 April 2003. It originally went into service on 18 October 1990. *Gavin Morrison*

*Below:* On 13 April 2001 No 91130, with no name or number, is shown passing Heck, the scene of the terrible accident on 28 February 2001. It is on the Doncaster test train after refurbishment, 10 days before it was released back into traffic numbered 91130 and named *City of Newcastle*. It originally entered BR stock on 6 March and was named *Palace of Holyrood House* on 26 June 1991, carrying it until May 1997. It is currently nameless. *Gavin Morrison*

*Left:* No 91111 *Terence Cuneo* passes Blindwalls, not far from the Scottish capital, with an express from King's Cross on 15 September 2004. It was the only member of the class to receive the National Express livery before the franchise was terminated in November 2009. It entered BR stock on 28 February 1990 and received its name on 3 March 1990, which it carried until May 1997. The name was reapplied in transfers in June 2000. *Gavin Morrison*

*Above:* No 91122 *Double Trigger* is at platform 5 at York ready to continue its journey north on the 9.00 King's Cross–Glasgow Central on 5 October 2007. Into stock on 3 October 1990, it was named *Robert Adley* from 17 November 1993 until March 1997, and then *Double Trigger* on 8 September 1999. Refurbishment was completed on 5 March 2002. *Gavin Morrison*

*Below:* The 12.40 Leeds–King's Cross passes Fitzwilliam with No 91117 *Cancer Research UK* at the south end of the coaches on 14 March 2007. It arrived at Bounds Green when new in July 1990, and was named *Commonwealth Institute* on 1 July 1993, which it carried until October 1996. Three years later, on 13 October 1999 it was named *City of Leeds*. It returned from refurbishment on 14 February 2002 and is currently named *West Riding Limited*. *Gavin Morrison*

*Above:* Alexander Palace sees No 91021 *Archbishop Thomas Cranmer* heading north with a down express from King's Cross at 4.16pm on 24 August 2000. It entered BR stock on 3 October 1990, but it was over five years before it was named *Royal Armouries* at Leeds station on 18 April 1996. When it was repainted into GNER colours in April 1997 the name was removed. It was released from refurbishment on 18 February 2003 with its name reapplied (it has since been removed). *Mike Mensing*

*Below:* On a perfect summer's day along the Northumberland coast, No 91115 *Holyrood* propels train 1E19, the 15.01 Edinburgh–King's Cross, past Spittal, just south of Tweedmouth, on 9 August 2007. It ran its first service on 9 June 1990, was named *Holyrood* on 10 November 1999 and was released from Doncaster after refurbishment on 16 August 2002. *Gavin Morrison*

*Above:* High above the River Tweed, No 91109 *The Samaritans* crosses the Royal Border Bridge on 9 August 2007. The bridge was designed by Robert Stephenson and Thomas E. Harrison, and opened in August 1850 by Queen Victoria. There are 28 arches with span dimensions of 61ft 6in and the rails are 126ft above the water level. The length is 2,152ft. *Gavin Morrison*

*Above:* The 16.10 King's Cross–Leeds races through Hadley Wood station headed by No 91107, now nameless, in what was intended to be a temporary National Express livery, and now East Coast colours. It entered service around the end of 1988 and received the name *Ian Allan* at Leeds station on 21 October 1993, which it carried until December 1996. It emerged from refurbishment on 4 April 2001 named *Newark on Trent. Mike Mensing*

*Below:* On 30 July 2008 the 11.50 Glasgow Central–King's Cross has No 91118 at the rear, running nameless with the temporary National Express branding, through New Barnet station. It worked its first service train on 28 July 1990. Named *Robert Louis Stevenson* on 30 November 1993 until May 1997. The name *Bradford Film Festival* followed on 17 February 2000, and it re-entered service after refurbishment on 26 November 2002. *Mike Mensing*

*Above:* Nameless No 91128, with white stripe with National Express, passes through the centre road at Doncaster station propelling the 1A36 14.56 Newcastle–King's Cross on 10 June 2008. *Gavin Morrison*

*Below:* No 91113, still with the white stripe but without National Express or East Coast branding, brings up the rear of the Sunday 13.24 Newcastle–King's Cross as it approaches Retford station on 20 September 2009. *Gavin Morrison*

*Above:* No 91111 was the only member of the class to receive the National Express livery. It is shown at the rear of an up express as it heads south past Doncaster on 30 September 2011. By this date it was running with East Coast in the white stripe rather than NEX but in November 2011 it was altered to the current East Coast livery. *Gavin Morrison*

*Below:* No 91101 and DVT NO 82205 were released during 2011 in this attractive livery to promote East Coast services, with the name *Flying Scotsman*. Needless to say it wasn't long before the locomotive and the DVT got separated and were seen running with the old GNER/NEX-liveried coaches. On 12 May 2012 it was running on the rear with an EC grey set as it headed south past Bridge 34 at Colton Junction near York. *Gavin Morrison*

*Above:* It is currently very rare to see Class 91s out on the main line working blunt end first. No 91106 in silver livery is passing Walefield Westgate station en route to Wabtec Works at Doncaster for attention on 24 July 2011. It is hauling a barrier vehicle from Neville Hill depot which was required at Doncaster. *Gavin Morrison*

*Below:* No 91107 was one of the few members of the class to receive the East Coast silver livery, before the decision was taken to adopt the grey colour. On 27 September 2011 it is passing Doncaster Black Carr on the 14.30 King's Cross-Newcastle, with GBRF No 66707 *Sir Sam Fay Great Central Railway* on the right, waiting to leave with a down coal train. *Gavin Morrison*

*Above:* No 91128 (currently nameless) has already featured in InterCity and GNER/National Express liveries. It is now in East Coast grey colours and at 10.35 on 5 September 2012 is seen leaving York. *Gavin Morrison*

*Below:* Class 91 No 91110 holds the speed record of 162mph for a UK locomotive, which it achieved on a test run on 17 September 1989. It was selected to attend the Railfest 2012 celebrations at the NRM at York, was decorated in special livery to commemorate the Battle of Britain and was named *Battle of Britain Memorial Flight.* The nameplate was in the same design as those attached to the famous Southern Railway 'Battle of Britain' class. The livery includes the motto 'Lest we forget' as well as images of Spitfire, Hurricane and Lancaster aircraft, which performed a flypast over the museum. Each side of the locomotive has a different aircraft image in the design. No 91110 is at the rear of the train in this photograph, passing Colton junction Bridge 33 on 9 September 2012. *Gavin Morrison*

# CLASS 92

**Numbered:** 92001-92046

**Built:** 1993-1996

**Number built:** 46

**Designed by:** Brush

**Constructed by:** Brush/ABB Zurich

**Weight:** 126 tons

**Continuous rated hp:** 6,760 25kv, 5,360 third rail 750V DC

**Max speed:** 87mph

**Withdrawn:** All still in service, although many have been in store

The Class 92s are undoubtedly the most complex and expensive locomotives ever to run over our network.

After the agreement to build the Channel Tunnel was made in 1987, decisions were soon taken on what trains would be needed. This resulted in the Class 373 'Eurostars', the Bo-Bo-Bos for the shuttle service and the Class 92 for freight.

The specification eventually issued by BR for the locomotives was extremely complex, partly due to the stringent safety features that had to be incorporated for working in the tunnel, plus they had to be suitable for third-rail 750V DC and 25kV overhead current collection.

Other features needing to be incorporated were the different signalling standards for either side of the channel, three different zones for fire protection and a virtual duplication of everything to ensure the locomotives could haul a train out of the tunnel if it failed, plus a myriad of other special features.

The body shells were built and painted by Procor at Wakefield and delivered to Brush at Loughborough.

Brecknell-Willis single arm pantographs were used for the 25kV and 12 pick-ups were attached to the bogies for the three-rail operation, with special devices to reduce arcing on the third rail.

A pair of three-phase asynchronous traction motors, 6PH type as used in the Shuttle locomotives, were installed, allowing 1,600 ton trains to be hauled, although in the tunnel anything over 1,300 tons was to be double-headed.

No 92001 was handed over to Rfd in February 1994, with deliveries completed on time in early 1996.

Their introduction into service proved to be very slow, many being stored upon completion. They were restricted to the third-rail-only areas on our network plus the tunnel services. Eventually they were allowed to work on the West Coast main line as far as Crewe and then to Mossend, and on the East Coast main line, although they are little used on this route. The six locomotives allocated to the 'Nightstar' services were used on common user duties (except No 92040) which was stored in 1997 and as at January 2011 has never entered service. All were put up for sale by Eurostar in 2000, but none were sold, so they have been in store until being refurbished in 2009 and 2010 for further use. Considering the complexity of the class they have performed well, but there has never been anything like enough work to keep the class fully occupied, and there are always some of the class in store.

No doubt they will continue to operate freight on the West Coast main line for many years to come.

*Right:* No 92016 is on display at Crewe International Electric Depot on 15 October 1994, when it was named *Brahms*. After the open day it was towed with No 92017 to MoD Kineton for storage, from where it emerged on 22 February 1995 and returned to Brush. It was also displayed at a Basford Hall open weekend on 27/28 August 1995, eventually entering service on 5 September 1995. *Gavin Morrison*

*Above:* Extensive testing was carried out with the Class 92s between Crewe and Carlisle Kingmoor yard, with trains running several times a week over a lengthy period. The test train with No 92005 *Mozart* at the rear has just arrived in the yard, No 92018 *Stendhal* having hauled it from Crewe, with No 92003 *Beethoven* in tow. The date of this picture was 22 November 1994, but No 92005 did not enter service till 10 August 1996. *Gavin Morrison*

*Right:* A view inside Brush Works at Loughborough on 3 May 1995 sees No 92014 *Emile Zola* receiving attention but not in service nine months after completion, after which it went back into store, before eventually being taken into stock on 24 September 1995. *Gavin Morrison*

*Left:*No 92016 *Brahms* at work on the West Coast main line with an up continental freight bound for Italy, taken at Old Linslade, just north of Leighton Buzzard, on 8 June 2005. *Gavin Morrison*

*Above:* A night shot of 92005 *Mozart* on display for an open day at Crewe Basford Hall yard. By this date, 20 August 1994, the locomotive was four months old, but did not enter service for another 26 months. *Gavin Morrison*

*Below:* Another open day at Crewe Basford Hall, 28 August 1995, where Nos 92023 *Ravel*, 92025 *Oscar Wilde* and 92036 *Bertolt Brecht* were on display. None of the three had entered service by this date, but did so within the next two months. *Gavin Morrison*

*Left:* Class 92s are occasionally used on railtours, which happened on 22 February 2003 with No 92031 *The Institute of Logistics and Transport.* It was one of two in the class (the other 92001) to receive EWS livery. This Pathfinder tour started at Crewe with a trip around London with electro-diesel Class 73s before No 92031 headed for Harwich, which was probably the first visit of the class to the port. It is seen passing Wrabness station on the outward journey. *Gavin Morrison*

*Right:* One of the five members of the class owned by SNCF (Société Nationale des Chémins de fer Français), No 92033 *Ravel* with SNCF logo is on common user duty as it heads an up freight past Winwick junction, just to the north of Warrington, on 4 March 2000. *Gavin Morrison*

*Left:* The other member of the class to receive EWS livery was No 92001 *Victor Hugo*, shown at the head of the 17.30 Wembley–Mossend, train No 6S77 as it passes Headstone Lane at 17.44 on its journey north on 26 May 2005. *Gavin Morrison*

*Above:* A very light freight passes through Kensington at 15.42 on 16 July 1996, heading east with No 92012 *Thomas Hardy*, a name once carried by a 'Britannia' Pacific. *Mike Mensing*

*Below:* No 92009 *Elgar* with Railfreight Distribution logos passes through the yard at the north end of Rugby with a short freight of cargo wagons on 30 October 2001. *Gavin Morrison*

*Above:* The 6X12 Mossend–Eastleigh passes Carlisle station at 17.26 on 1 May 2002 headed by No 92036 *Bertolt Brecht*. The locomotive spent a considerable amount of time out of use in late 2003 and 2004. *Gavin Morrison*

*Below:* In 2005 EWS decided to apply stickers to all its locomotives which had not received the maroon livery. Here No 92025 *Oscar Wilde* rounds the curve between Low Gill and Beckfoot, heading the 9.05 4M63 Mossend to Chirk log train which it will work as far as Warrington. On 24 July 2006 the loading hardly required the 6,760hp of the Class 92. *Gavin Morrison*

*Above:* Before it received its distinctive 'Stobart' livery, No 92017, then named *Shakespeare*, is near Burton on Holme heading the 6X12 17.20 Carlisle–Eastleigh freight on 21 May 2007. *Gavin Morrison*

*Below:* Another view of the 6X12, this time passing through the scenic Lune Gorge headed by No 92015 *D. H. Lawrence* on 2 May 2007. *Gavin Morrison*

*Above:* A side-on view of No 92007 *Schubert* heading an up freight at 13.40 past Crawford on 6 September 2005. It was completed in June 1994 but didn't enter service until September 1996. *P. Corrie*

*Below:* In superb winter conditions on 8 January 2010, No 92017, in the Stobart livery and named *Bart the Engine,* heads the 4Z48, the 10.00 Carlisle–Rugby, past Docker with the Westmoreland hills in the background. *Gavin Morrison*

*Above:* No 92032 was originally named *Cesar Frank* when it was part of the Eurostar fleet of Class 92s. It has now lost the name and is currently the only member of the class to be in the GBRF blue livery. The ex-Eurostar locomotives spent many years in store and are now part of Eurotunnel. No 92032 is now on hire to GBRF and on 14 July 2011 is seen passing Long Buckby on the 19.07 4092 Daventry-Dollonds Moor Norfolk Line Intermodel. *J. Turner*

*Below:* No 92009 *Marco Polo* has already featured on page 92 but it is now shown in the smart DB Schenker red livery. It is seen heading the 6M76 21.36 Mossend-Wembley empty china clay tanks past Linslade on 25 May 2012. *J. Turner*

# AFTERLIFE

*Above:* Although No 86101 was withdrawn in December 2001, it became the first of the class to return to the main line in preservation. It has done relatively little work since late 2007, except in early 2008 when it was used on weekend workings on the East Coast main line to help out Hull Trains who were short of Class 222s. It has retained its name *Sir William A. Stanier FRS* and has been painted in BR blue livery. It is shown passing Marnholm near Peterborough on an empty stock working for Hull Trains' 5G02, the 12.33 Doncaster–Bounds Green on 27 January 2008. *J. Turner*

*Below:* Class 86/7 No 86701 *Orion* in the attractive silver and red livery of Electric Traction Services heads north past Greenholm hauling a couple of Class 325 Royal Mail EMUs on the Warrington–Shieldmuir working on 8 January 2010. No 86701 was formerly Class 86/2 No 86205 *City of Lancaster* and also carried the numbers E3129 and 86503. No 86702 *Cassiopeia* (ex-No 86260, 86048 and E3144) is also passed for main-line running, but to date (2012) have seen little work. *P. Corrie*